Biscuitville

Best wishes!

Burney Jennings

To the Biscuitville family, whose business behavior serves as a beacon of hope for a better corporate tomorrow.

THE SECRET RECIPE
FOR BUILDING A
SUSTAINABLE
COMPETITIVE ADVANTAGE

J. PHILLIPS L. JOHNSTON

EASTON
STUDIO PRESS

infiniteideas

Copyright © J. Phillips L. Johnston, 2009

The right of J. Phillips L. Johnston to be identified as the author of this book has been asserted in accordance with the Copyright, Designs and Patents Act 1988.

First published in 2009 by

Infinite Ideas Limited
36 St Giles
Oxford
OX1 3LD
United Kingdom
www.infideas.com

Easton Studio Press
PO Box 3131
Westport
CT 06880, USA
(203) 454 4454
www.eastonsp.com

A CIP catalogue record for this book is available from the British Library

UK ISBN 978–1–906821–10–4

US ISBN 978-1-935212-05-8

Brand and product names are trademarks or registered trademarks of their respective owners.

Designed and typeset by Baseline Arts Ltd, Oxford
Printed and bound in Canada

Contents

Foreword

All throughout the developed world, the corporate community has lost its way. Greed manifested in short-term, quarterly earnings games at the expense of long-term achievement and the lack of leadership in C-suites are at the top of the list of causes.

If the Enrons and Tycos were the left jabs in a high-stakes Wall Street prize fight, then highfalutin derivatives, no equity sub-prime mortgages with their built-in interest rate grenades, and gamblers like Bernie Madoff betting billions of dollars of OPM (other people's money) were body blows to the solar plexus, causing immeasurable pain to the public trust. Flotsam and jetsam from the backwash of such investment shenanigans will sully financial shores for years to come. The worldwide scene is reminiscent of the all-nighters in *The Great Gatsby*.

The result is the Great Recession of 2009. It is worldwide, its roots are insidious and history will measure it in years, not quarters. How does the corporate world restore this dashed public trust? We know first-hand that the master legislation named Sarbanes–Oxley in the U.S., and legislation similar to it in other developed countries, has in most cases been an abject failure.

Furthermore, smart money says governments that are becoming more and more the masters of big business will not be the restorers of public trust (or, for that matter, the bottom line).

We need to acknowledge that the fix is not in more legislation. Morals and values cannot be legislated; it will not be management by governments that instills probity. Instead, we offer these pages as alternatives, if not answers, to the restoration of public trust using the uniqueness and soundness of Biscuitville's business recipe (pun intended):

◆ Ethics by example of business leaders. Eschew written ethics policies; live the sermon.

◆ Make decisions with a long-term horizon. Private companies like Biscuitville have a built-in advantage over public companies with 10Q realities.

◆ Work for, not against, social reform.

◆ Include community and neighborhoods as stakeholders.

◆ Focus on civic order.

◆ Empower entrepreneurship and soft leadership skills.

◆ Afford all employees respect, not just vertically but horizontally. "People first" philosophy, when extended to customers, leads to a sustainable competitive advantage.

In short, business must get back to fundamentals, which Biscuitville, unlike its larger public cousins, never abandoned. Biscuitville has smartly avoided leverage and deal making over

Biscuitville

its long history, concentrating on active management with rolled-up sleeves. All employees are, in fact, their brother's keeper, even during the storms of business and of life.

Biscuitville is a worthy template for restoring trust in business everywhere.

———➤●◄———

I would like to express my gratitude to Charlotte Liebig for her incisive editing and for inspiring me throughout the writing of this volume, not only as my editor but also as my long-standing personal friend.

Chapter 1

Gitcha a biscuit...

In the midst of the worst recession in seventy-five years, with trust in business even lower than it was after Enron and the dot-com bust, admiration for the corporate world is in short supply.

On the other hand, those few companies in the world that practice homespun ethics, the seemingly rare few that nurture, develop, train, and treat employees with enduring respect, and the fewer still that are jealously protective of their reputations among employees, community, and the marketplace, deserve to be admired. Any company that continues to perform well ethically, maintain its good name, and preserve its profitability during what could be called "The Great Recession" of the early twenty-first century will be more admired than the high-octane performers of the boom times. It was precisely because those companies lacked high ethical standards that so many of them faltered and collapsed when the economy began to unravel.

Superior ethical standards are the norm at Biscuitville and are precisely why this vital and growing forty-three-year-young company will exit the gloomy post-recessionary tunnel with more market share, greater employee loyalty, a balance sheet as impenetrable and strong as the Rock of Gibraltar, a highly recognizable brand within their footprint, and a sustainable competitive advantage that is the envy of many of its competitors. Biscuitville is admired by and involved in each of the communities it serves, and its corporate philanthropy is well respected. Biscuitville is a beacon of light in a period of epic economic darkness. And the reason? A loyal customer base coupled with the best biscuits south of the Mason–Dixon line. By what standard should Biscuitville be measured as it lays claim to the top spot on the podium of best quick-serve restaurants? How can Biscuitville, as it surpasses the one-thousand employee mark in 2010, lay claim to becoming one of *Fortune* magazine's Best 100 Companies to Work For®? Read on. Biscuitville has all it takes to make that coveted list. The ultimate business thermometer is return on investment (ROI). It will tell you if a company is sick or healthy. Comparing Biscuitville, an Internal Revenue Service (IRS) Section 1372 subchapter S private company (where income is taxed directly to the stockholders), to the *Fortune* 100 companies might seem a stretch, since all the current 100 are public companies. But with Biscuitville's pre-tax ROI reaching a high of 58.7% and a low of 40.8% over the last five years, Biscuitville can rightfully claim the ROI gold medal against the most ferocious *Fortune* 100 competitors on the planet. A more impressive measurement is Biscuitville's employment scorecard: Biscuitville has never had a company-wide lay-off in its history; it has never furloughed any crew. Lay-offs and furloughs have long-term cost consequences beyond merely the severance costs. Morale suffers horribly. Survivors' medical costs spike due to stress, especially concern about job retention. Rehiring and retraining expenses cut into profits. And there is always the possibility that future high-performance C-level executives are swept out in the cuts. "People capital" is an undervalued and unappreciated asset. It is difficult to measure the value of the human resource from a cost–benefit perspective. At Biscuitville, people relationships – the "people first" philosophy – are more important than corporate mission. Who is on the bus (people) is more important than where the bus is going (mission). That's what makes this company tick. All employees learn about the importance of respecting each other. And respect goes in all directions, not just vertically: top to bottom, side to side, and out to the customers.

Biscuitville

Workplace bullying is an epidemic. According to a 2007 comprehensive survey, more than fifty-four million American workers reported being bullied at work. Workplace violence or rudeness is unthinkable at Biscuitville, where employees are simply asked to treat each other and customers with the common courtesy people have a right to expect of one another. Biscuitville has achieved the Holy Grail sought by all businesses: a sustainable competitive advantage (SCA). It has done so through extraordinary service but with a twist. Because they are treated so well, customers keep coming back. Biscuitville's remarkable level of service gives it a sustainable competitive advantage superior to patent holders like Cisco; to low-price producers like Wal-Mart; to differentiators, like Rolex, and even to a revered trademark like Coke. By building its brand and investing in its employees, Biscuitville has attained a level of profitability to be envied.

Many innovative business concepts will be explored in these pages. The lifestory of Maurice Jennings provides insight into why "Founder" is the most important title in business. His son, Burney Jennings, teaches how soft power leadership produces hard dollars as an emerging company matures. Old concepts and archaic ways of analyzing employee psychology will be dusted off and given a shiny new layer of understanding, much to the relief of beleaguered and undervalued employees. Maslow's Hierarchy of Needs is out; meeting employee needs is in. This was echoed when Johnson & Johnson was named in the annual listing of the *Fortune* 100 Best Companies to Work For® in March 2009: CEO Bill Weldon said that the most important thing his company is doing is "helping employees recognize that we're going to continue to invest in them and their development." That concept is nothing new at Biscuitville. Private ownership of companies that have cherry-picked the best practices of the Sarbanes–Oxley Act trumps public company ownership in today's business world. The expression "the best of all worlds" describes a company, like Biscuitville, that is private, profitable, accountable, and well on the way to the transparency required by the law's new ethical standards for public companies. And it has become so voluntarily. At Biscuitville communication is by action. The Jennings family teaches ethics, and senior management lives righteously. Behavior trickles down: no pomp, no words, "Just do it." And it gets done. The pay-off is happy employees and an even happier bottom line.

So sit back. Imagine that Troy has just been defeated, and you are starting out on a forty-three-year odyssey to observe Founder Maurice Jennings' vision, to witness Biscuitville's dough-making (yes, pun intended), and to understand how Biscuitville achieved a Steinway-esque reputation "without all the hoopla."

As they say in the South, "Gitcha a biscuit...", and if you want the best of the best, get it from Biscuitville.

Chapter 2

The color of winter

On January 24, 2008 the pewter fingers of dawn captured the city of Martinsville in ruins. Like Richmond, the capitol of the Confederacy in 1865, Martinsville has been through a war – an economic war which has left all its buildings standing, but some are nothing but dark and empty shells standing against a hueless sky, testaments to businesses once flourishing but long since departed.

Cheap foreign labor is the weapon of mass destruction that has emptied the city of its prosaic textile, furniture, and manufacturing industries, including familiar household names like Bassett and Fieldcrest. A battered pick-up truck limps up the street against a backdrop of brown dirt hills. Through a crack in the side window, the doleful wail of a country tune beats against the ears of a few unintended listeners on the street. If only country music could be played backwards, songs could end happily: Ole' Earl would get his dog and wife back and not always end up wrapped in a tarpaulin in the trunk of a convertible.

The spidery silhouette of broad-leaf trees, lacking their foliage, adds to the city's frosty dreariness. A stray mottled brown mutt scrounges for food, wet nose sniffing icy gray pavement. It's cold: twenty degrees. It's winter in Virginia. Martinsville is a stop on the Nascar racing circuit, a popular annual event, but mostly people pass through here on their way to tourist destinations like the near-by Blue Ridge Mountains or south to bigger cities like Charlotte, North Carolina.

Fade in to the hum of the gathering breakfast crowd at 1706 Virginia Avenue (Store Number 119 to Biscuitville's 941 employees). In sharp contrast to the flows of pewter outside, the bright yellow storefront invites customers to come in from the cold. The look and smell of the best biscuits anywhere in these parts provides a welcome visual and olfactory oasis from the gloom.

Tonia Pegram, the store's manager, greets me cheerfully and sits down in one smooth practiced motion. Her Doris Day good looks and "Golden Retriever" personality (characterized by an abiding eagerness to help and please others) serve as a homespun mood elevator. We begin to talk about her life and career.

The two are so intermingled it is difficult to tell where the line between life and career is. Tonia speaks affectionately of her husband Greg and her two teenage children, wistfully musing, "Little girls grow up too soon and leave your side." In almost the same breath, she reminisces about her twenty-three years at Biscuitville, frequently intermingling stories of home and business as she recounts her experiences. Tonia is both a part of her family and part of another – the Biscuitville "family." As it is with her crew, so it is with customers. All are part of the Biscuitville "family." Tonia is particularly eager to tell how her crew recently befriended a customer with no family who had been diagnosed with terminal cancer. In a gesture of compassion, the crew rallied support in order to give comfort to the down-and-out in their community. That's how it's done at Biscuitville. It's not just about the biscuits.

She tells me of her personal goals for her career at Biscuitville: making the best biscuits, providing the best customer service, and making Biscuitville even better for fellow employees. "I did it with no increase in my budget," she delights like a child, her smile a ray of bright sunshine clashing with the roiling dreariness outside.

Tonia becomes even more animated as she tells the story of her supervisor, Brenda Long. Brenda started with the company in 1983 as the early morning biscuit-maker at the old Biscuitville on Church Street in Burlington, North Carolina. Late in 1983 Brenda was promoted to Shift Leader. The same year she was promoted to Assistant Manager. In 1987 she was promoted to Operator. In 2000, she was moved to one of the top senior positions, that of District Supervisor, earning one of the company's top salaries.

Tonia proudly lavishes praise on Brenda's management skills, especially her respect for her fellow employees and her listening ability. Great managers know how to draw out and assimilate information without interrupting. Truly listening, without simultaneously formulating what to say next, is rare. As they say in the South, "Don't go talkin' when you should be lis'nin."

Brenda is the poster child for upward mobility; a walking definition of opportunity; the personification of the chance to rise in rank regardless of the race, sex, circumstances – you name it – into which you were born. Individual opportunity abounds at Biscuitville: seventy-six per cent of the 941 employees are female, and fifty-six per cent are from ethnic minority groups. Brenda, who is both female and from an ethnic minority, had the intelligence, guts, and drive to earn the senior management rank of District Supervisor over thirteen stores and 235 employees. Her "can do" spirit and "anything is possible" determination are infectious. Brenda is a celebration of the self-made person. At Biscuitville one's destiny is shaped by way of motivation, smartness, and hard work. Brenda Long, with her grit and spunk, serves as a role model and paves the way for other ambitious, determined young people.

In addition to devoted employees like Tonia and Brenda, the true secret recipe, alongside the melt-in-your-mouth biscuits, is the respect Biscuitville shows each employee and, in turn, the respect employees show each other. Most companies are savvy enough to show respect to their customers. Rare is the company whose employees respect each other. Half of working Americans (forty-nine per cent) have suffered or witnessed workplace bullying – including verbal abuse, job sabotage, abuse of authority, or destruction of workplace relationships, according to the 2007 Workplace Bullying Institute/Zogby Interactive survey, the largest such survey ever conducted on the subject. We have all witnessed employee abuse of fellow employees.

Such disgraceful conduct in the workplace is widespread. Disrespect and incivility by employees toward fellow employees exacts a heavy cost. Greatly tempered by the boss–worker structure, even those in formal work relationships call for a tablespoon of respect.

Biscuitville's customer-service model is a mysterious rarity in the corporate world: customers are extended the very same respect the employees receive from and give to each other. Do unto customers as has been done unto you. This credo emanates from the top of the Biscuitville organization, and extends out into the community it serves. The impact of Biscuitville's credo has resulted in a wonderful success story. What makes that story even more impressive is that Biscuitville has put together enviable financial credentials with no outside investment or debt on its balance sheet. Public companies' financials, in comparison, are lackluster aside those of private Biscuitville.

Biscuitville will explore how Maurice Jennings was a visionary serial entrepreneur, and the reasons why CEO Burney Jennings and his Biscuitville cadre of happy employees have been so outstanding in the fast-food industry simply by consistently making fluffy, delicious, golden homemade biscuits. These biscuits, unrivaled in their taste and appeal, consistently served up on a golden platter of excellent, personalized customer service, has yielded extraordinary success at a time when quick-service giants are struggling to be profitable, and poor performance is the norm.

Biscuitville is an example of innovative leadership, enlightened business ethics, and consistently high standards of customer service, resulting in a sustainable competitive advantage (SCA). These same business methodologies are the reasons why private ownership trumps public ownership.

In exploring why this Southern company has enjoyed such enormous success, the best place to start is, of course, at the beginning. The next chapter tells the story of Biscuitville and its Southern roots.

Chapter 3

Brother got the farm

Family

Mother was the hero. When I was a boy summertimes were spent with my grandparents on a middle Tennessee farm. My grandmother made big buttermilk biscuits like we make at Biscuitville. She would give me an extra one at lunch to put in the middle front pocket of my overalls and take to the field. It tasted pretty good about four o'clock in the afternoon.

My mother's family was from Newnan, Georgia, about thirty miles southwest of Atlanta. My granddaddy died in the flu epidemic of 1918 when my mother was eight. He had a small grocery store on the town square. My sixteen-year-old uncle tried to keep the store open, but it was too much for him. So when he got work in Atlanta, he moved his mother and five sisters to Atlanta, where there were better job opportunities for all of them. Most of them lived there the rest of their lives. My dad's family was from middle Tennessee out from Murfreesboro. My grandparents were farmers. They were born less than twenty years after the end of the Civil War. The north destroyed most of the infrastructure of the south, including schools. The south lost more than a generation of educated populace. I don't know how much education our grandparents had. I do know neither one of them went to college.

In the early part of the twentieth century, they scratched out an existence on a marginal farm. They did not have electricity (lights, refrigeration, or running water) until the Tennessee Valley Authority brought power to their part of Tennessee in the 1930s. The first thing Granddad did every morning was start the wood stove in the kitchen. He did that even after they got an electric stove. Then he went to the barn to milk the cows. They separated the milk and sold the cream to a dairy. They fed the skim milk to the hogs.

Nanny washed dishes in plain water first and put that water in the hog slop. Then she washed with soap. She caught rainwater to wash their clothes. They grew and sold wheat and corn. They raised most of what they ate in the garden, the orchard, and livestock. They canned vegetables and fruit and cured pork in the summer. They belonged to a beef and a pork club. The club slaughtered a cow or a pig periodically, and the club members shared the meat.

They raised their own chickens and harvested eggs. They exchanged most of the eggs for groceries in town, usually on Saturday. They cut ice from the lake in the winter and stored it in sawdust in the wellspring, and had some ice in the spring, summer, and fall. Nanny made her own soap. She made most of their clothes.

During WWII the army conducted maneuvers in middle Tennessee because the terrain is similar to France. Occasionally, Nanny would cook meals for soldiers in the home to make extra money. The maneuvers did a lot of damage to the farmland, but the farmers were compensated. When Granddad saw a convoy coming he would go out to meet them and ask where they were going and lead them through the farm, if necessary. Otherwise, they would cut right across and mow down anything in sight.

Nanny's maiden name was Bass, and she had one sister that I knew. She called her sister Hattie, which was short for Harriet (her married name was Brown). Hattie had five chldren, Milan, Ivan, Randolph, Wilson and Alice. Nanny also had a brother or brothers that I never knew. I understand they all died of hypertension and strokes. She must have been one of the youngest in her family.

Granddad had five siblings, Herbert, Herman, Bertin, Deni, and Dessie Mae. Dessie Mae married Willie Mike Flowers and had four children: Wilson David, Lawrence Henry, Albert Sherrill and Lynette. Herbert and his wife, Era Mae, had a farm similar to our grandparents', close by. They had one son, Lee, who died at twenty-five playing baseball. Herman married Lulu Price Greer and moved to western Tennessee. I never knew his wife. They had one daughter named Marion Palace Jennings. When I lived with Nanny and Granddad in the summers, we used to go visiting on Sunday afternoons, unannounced. We almost never went to the same place twice, and most of the people we visited were kin.

During the winters my granddad, dad, and uncle went to Chicago to work in the paper mills for extra money. My dad took a secretarial course at Cumberland College in Cumberland, Kentucky, and after graduating went to Atlanta to get work. He worked in distribution for *The Atlanta Journal*. While there he met my mother, and they were married in 1930. Through a friend he got a job with Valier & Speas flour milling company in St. Louis, selling bakery flour in Georgia. Later, he got a job with International Milling Company selling bakery flour in North Carolina. We moved to Greensboro in 1938 when I was four years old.

Early years

Before my sister Janice was born in the summer of 1938, I went to stay with my grandparents for a while. When my dad came to get me I did not want to go home because I liked living on the farm. My dad made an agreement with me. We would pack my clothes, get in the car, and drive down the lane across the field in front of the house where we would stop. If I wanted to stay for the rest of the summer, I could get out of the car and walk back to the house. And that's what I did. Nanny said many times she remembered me coming across the field back to her house dragging my suitcase. I went to my grandparents' farm every summer for several years after that. I worked on the farm and learned what it was like to be a farmer: milked cows every morning, fed the hogs, cut wheat, harvested corn.

I started school at Lindley Elementary in Greensboro in 1940. David Brown and I were classmates. We had the same teacher, Mrs. Booker, for the first and second grade. They must have been short of classrooms and teachers because they took our brightest classmates, mostly girls, and skipped them a grade from the second to the fourth grade. David said it was a couple of years before he realized what had happened.

My dad bought an interest in a bakery in Burlington, North Carolina, in 1941, so we moved from Greensboro to Burlington. The bakery had a retail store and about a half-dozen wholesale routes. The first Christmas there I worked setting up carryout boxes. I could pretty much eat all of the bakery products I wanted. So while nobody paid much attention, I ate about three-dozen doughnuts in one day. I did not eat another doughnut for two years.

I worked in the bakery a lot during that time because help was so hard to get during the Second World War. A lot of women also worked in the bakery during the war, which was unusual. I also did the usual adolescent things – played football and baseball, etc. I was never very good at either one. I'm lucky they kept me on the teams. When Charlie "Choo Choo" Justice was playing football for Carolina I use to thumb to Chapel Hill for every game. I'd wait until they played *The Star Spangled Banner* and for the police to salute at attention, and then I would climb the fence and watch the game standing up inside. Most people stood up when Carolina was on offense anyway.

A bunch of us formed a boxing club called "The Blue Streak Boxing Club." The name came from the fact that when we tried to print tickets for a boxing match in my basement there was a blue streak from the printer on the tickets. We staged boxing matches in my basement. Lace Hall, who is in the North Carolina Boxing Hall of Fame, was our star. We didn't make much money. A local businessman had gotten the franchise for the Tucker Torpedo automobiles and built a building. The Tucker Torpedo did not work out, so I rented his car-wash area and organized a group of us to wash cars on the weekends. I did make a little money out of that.

I remember always having a paper route from the time I was about twelve years old. In fact, most of the time I had two routes. I delivered the Greensboro paper in the morning and the Burlington paper in the afternoon, both along a similar route. I had to get up at 5:30 a.m. for the morning route because the papers had to be delivered by 7:00 a.m. I would deliver every day and collect once a week. I caused quite a furor when I told my customers we were changing procedures and collecting once a month instead of once a week. A lot of my customers didn't want to pay once a month. My brother, R.B., would help me on the route, especially when I was out of town. Dad's bakery did pretty well. However, he had a disagreement with his partner and sold his interest in 1948. He went into the bakery ingredients brokerage business selling bakery ingredients on commission. At that time it took about two years to get started in the brokerage business; he suffered a stroke in 1950 two years after he started. He was forty-two years old and was never able to work after that. I was fifteen, my sister Janice was eleven and my brother, R.B., Jr., was nine. All of the money from the sale of the bakery had been spent. I worked in restaurants during that time because they were some of the few places that would hire young people. It was fairly easy to get a job. I also worked in a movie theatre, clothing store, radio station, and on a farm.

Biscuitville

One of my first jobs was working at Roy's Drive-In on South Church Street when I was fifteen years old. Roy lived in Raleigh and wasn't making any money at the drive-in. So he sent his accountant to Burlington to work for a week to try to see what the problem was. He got a room just up the street in a rooming house. I was working the third shift, 11:00 p.m. to 7:00 a.m., and mopped the floor about 5 o'clock in the morning. I forgot and left the mop bucket right outside the front door. This morning, instead of walking out to the sidewalk, the accountant felt pretty good and came down toward the drive-in jumping the hedgerows. He jumped right into the mop bucket.

One summer I went to Carolina Beach and worked in restaurants and a bingo parlor. During the school year I usually worked as a staff announcer at the local radio station WBBB (We Build Better Burlington).

In the summer when I was eighteen I thumbed to Kansas and worked the wheat harvest driving a truck. I carried my clothes with me and slept wherever I could find a place to lie down, which was usually on the wheat in the bed of the truck. They paid $1.50 an hour - $1.00 in cash and 50 cents at the end of the season if you stayed with them to the end of the harvest. While I was out there I met a couple of guys from Los Angeles, Frank Small, and Tom Smith. Tom had a car, and I rode home with them and stayed with Frank for a couple of days and saw some of Los Angeles. We still keep in touch.

After my senior year in high school I figured if I was going to college I'd better get on with it. I went to Elon College near Burlington and talked with Dean Hook. He told me to come on up and we'd see how it worked out. So I did. About that time Johnny Loy and I opened a short-order restaurant in an existing restaurant building owned by his dad. I don't remember what we named it. We had about fifteen counter seats with counter service only. The health department closed us down because we did not keep the place clean. I never forgot that lesson.

Elon was on the quarter system at the time. I attended one quarter and joined the Air Force for various reasons. I was sent to Lackland Air Force Base in San Antonio, Texas. From there I went into pilot training. I failed flight school from lack of interest and went to Warren Air Force Base in Cheyenne, Wyoming. In Cheyenne we also did "troop" shows which was a lot of fun. You'd be surprised how much talent there was at our base.

From there I went to Far East Air Force Headquarters in Tokyo. All the while I worked in the Office of Information Services, which handled media – radio, television, and newspapers – for the bases. I wrote, produced, and handled radio and television programs, and wrote for the newspapers.

The only night I ever spent in jail was one time when I was thumbing from San Antonio to Burlington in the Air Force. I was somewhere in Georgia about 2:00 a.m. There was no traffic. I saw a police station and walked in. I was in Air Force uniform and asked if they had anywhere I could sleep. The sergeant said I could sleep in one of the cells, so I went back there and sacked in. That's the story of the only night I ever spent in jail.

In 1955, after six months in Japan, I got a hardship discharge and came back home to try to save the family sales business. After his stroke, my dad could not talk, so my mother traveled with him to talk for him and try to sell bakery ingredients. When I came back to work with him, my mother stayed home and ran the office while I tried to develop the flour part of the business, which was the most profitable.

Early business

We did fairly well. Our first year's commission was $5,000. That became $10,000, then $15,000 and went on up from there. Out of that we had to travel and live as best we could. My brother, R.B., still has the flour business, and he sells a lot of flour, more than I ever did. However, the high point of my flour brokerage career was when I sold twenty-five bargeloads of flour to Kern's Bakery in Knoxville, Tennessee. A bargeload is fifteen rail cars. The commission was $15,000, and that was a lot of money in those days.

When Patricia Gordon and I were married in 1957, two families had to live on the profits of the brokerage business. Patricia and I had three children: Mary Nell was born in 1959, Fran in 1961, and Burney in 1963. Mary Nell had microcephaly. Her brain did not grow. She had an abnormally small head. We kept her at home until just before Fran was born and then put her in an institution that cares for children like her. We transferred her to a North Carolina state institution when she was six years old. She has been in an institution all of her life. Fran is a homemaker in Charlotte. She and her husband, Chris, have two children named Tricia and Gordon. Burney is President and CEO of Biscuitville. He and his wife, Dina, have four children named Blake, Bailey, Mary Frances, and John.

My dad died in 1962. I traveled all over the East selling bakery flour. I bought my first airplane, a Beechcraft Bonanza, in 1962 and used it in the business. Later, I bought a Beechcraft Baron, which we used in the restaurant business mainly to find and visit suppliers. We still have a small interest in a Beechcraft King Air, which we use in our business. I enjoyed flying and used our airplanes well in our businesses. However, I do not encourage anybody to take up flying. It is dangerous compared to professional flying, and it takes a lot of time to learn to fly, especially instrument flying. During that time I saved $30,000, enough to start another business – Pizza-To-Go.

Pizza-To-Go

One of my flour prospects was L.S. Hartzog in Memphis. He
owned Hart's Bakeries. He had opened bread stores in St. Louis
selling fresh bread at wholesale prices. That was the first thing
I had seen that looked better than the flour brokerage
business, so I decided to go into the bread store business. We
opened our first two bread stores on October 4, 1966, in
Burlington, one on North Church Street and the other on East
Webb Avenue. On the first day there were six of us – me, Max
Fogleman, a supervisor, and four cashiers. I still remember it
like it was yesterday. We had room in the store that we didn't
need, so we put in pizza to go. Pizza was just getting started in
the south at that time, and it was very popular. In fact, the
pizza was more popular than the bread, so we took the bread
out and kept the pizza.

McDonald's made the restaurant business respectable. Until
McDonald's franchised and made some
businessmen/franchisees wealthy, the restaurant business was
usually a one- or two-person business where the owners,
usually husband and wife, worked most of the time. But I
remember sitting in a restaurant one time with my uncle
Maurice, and he looked around and said, "This is a good
business." I said, "What business?" He said, "This business, the
restaurant business." I said, "You have to be there all the time."

He said, "Have you ever been in a Howard Johnson's?" I said, "Yes". He said, "Have you ever seen Howard Johnson there?" I said, "Point well taken!"

Anyway, we were into pizza-to-go. We put in picnic benches for seats. We served pizza at the counter. We had a vending machine for drinks. I caught a lot of flack from my family and friends about that. Later, we put in a drink fountain and tea and coffee. We still called it Pizza-To-Go. At first we bought all of the ingredients ready to assemble and bake the pizzas. I remember the first time we bought bulk pepperoni I opened the box and said, "How do you cut this stuff?" An employee said, "I've got a pocket knife." I said, "Whip it out." He did and started sawing on the end of the pepperoni. I said, "This ain't going to work." So we bought a slicing machine with a cylinder, loaded the pepperoni and sliced it. It was a "slow" winter. So "slow" that we closed the store on East Webb Avenue and concentrated on North Church Street. We had closed down half of our restaurants. During this time I kept up my flour sales because the restaurant was not profitable yet. I still managed the Pizza-To-Go.

In the spring business started picking up, so I hired my first manager, Jack King, a high-school classmate with a lot of restaurant experience. Jack once told me things were "picking up." He said they came and "picked up" his television, "picked up" his car. He said things were really "picking up." He always had something like that to say. And he still does.

About that time a guy opened a steak house called The Peddler in Greensboro. He opened at 6:00 p.m. and closed at 10:00 p.m. He sold rib-eye steak cut to order with a salad bar, baked potato, and bread. He also had some desserts. That looked like a good idea, so I opened one on South Church Street in Burlington in an old "Three Pigs of America" building. At first we called it The Patrician then changed the name to The Cutting Board and operated it for thirty-five years until it burned in 2004. By that time I had had the steak house half of my life. I never cried about it, but I came close. After we took the building down I rode over to the lot and sat there thinking. It was sad but it was over. Some fellows in Burlington bought the rights to The Cutting Board and have reopened it close to where it was originally.

There are a couple of interesting stories about The Cutting Board. When we bought the lot to put it on, there was a house there. We borrowed as much money on it as we could. Later, we wanted to move the house to make room for more parking. So I went to see Walter Cooper at Community Federal. I said, "Walter, you know I've got a loan on the house next to The

Cutting Board." He said, "You're telling me. I haven't been able to sleep since I made that loan." I said, "Walter, I want to move the house to another lot." He thought a minute. Then he said, "Tell you what, Maurice. You write me a check for the balance of the loan, and I will put it right here in my desk drawer. You keep on making the payments and move the house. When you have the house ready to live in call me, and I will bring the 'committee' out to inspect the house. Then I'll give you your check back." And that's what we did. Pretty nice! I don't think they do business that way now.

Also, when we built The Cutting Board we only built half as many seats as we would eventually want. When I was ready to add the rest of the building I went to see the building inspector. I said, "John, I'm ready to build the rest of The Cutting Board." He said, "Are you going to build it like the original?" I said, "Yes". He said, "Go ahead and build it." Later he brought me a building permit and did his usual inspections during construction. Wayne Bunting called on us from Kraft Foods. I saw his talent and talked him into coming to Burlington to run The Cutting Board. Later, I got him to run all of our restaurants. He did a good job. He eventually left us to start his own restaurant chain, Blue Ribbon Grills.

The restaurant business is a sales business. By that I mean, as sales go up costs do not go up as fast, so you make more money. Our first pizza restaurants did $700 to $800 a week. When we opened in Battleground Avenue in Greensboro we did $1800 a week, and I thought that was great. We were getting better. Later, we reorganized our restaurants and added spaghetti and a salad bar. We had become a quick-service restaurant, which did not fit the name Pizza-To-Go, so we changed the name from Pizza-To-Go to Pizzaville and expanded to ten units.

Pizzaville

When I went into the restaurant business I traveled a lot, finding supplies and looking at other restaurants. Anytime I heard of an interesting restaurant or restaurant concept I got in the plane and flew there to take a look for myself. I also did a lot of driving. One time Hal Hassenfelt, our supervisor, and I left Burlington and drove to Atlanta stopping and eating at various "different" restaurants we had heard about. We had planned to spend the night in Atlanta, but, after supper I said, "I don't want to spend the night here." He said he didn't either, so, we drove back to Burlington and got to bed about 4:00 in the morning. We bought our tomato products and a lot of our ingredients from a wholesale supplier. Early one spring our supplier told me they would not have any more tomato products until summer when a new crop of tomatoes would be harvested, so I went out and found and bought enough tomato products to last us until the new harvest. I decided that if I was going to have to do that we might as well make some money on it, so we began distributing our own products. We still distribute everything our Biscuitvilles need except fresh produce and dairy products. There are many advantages to this, including controlling our costs and not having various suppliers in the Biscuitvilles. Working closely with our distributing company is our repair and maintenance department. We want all of our restaurants to be repaired immediately and all of our restaurants to look like they have just been remodeled.

In 1972 I enrolled in Elon College again for two years and took about every business course they offered. Later, I served on the Board of Trustees for twenty years. I retired in 1999. My son, Burney, graduated from Elon in 1985 and serves on the Board now.

Early on, when we were remodeling buildings and building restaurants, I would be at the contractors and sub-contractors before they went to work to see if they were going to show up and what they were going to do that day. I never felt I could ask builders to do something and depend on them doing it. I always felt I had to follow up. Bob Burton, a Chicago restaurant designer, did most of our early design work. I got on to Bob through Jim Prentiss who ran Shoney's South with his cousin, Terry Young. One day I called Jim and asked him who was the best restaurant designer in the country. He said he didn't know, but that Bob Burton did his work. I told him that was what I was asking.

Bob Anderson, who had worked in marketing with McDonald's, was also instrumental in our restaurant design. Bob said our building should be our sign. When people see our building from a distance they should recognize the shape and color and know it is ours. With pizza, spaghetti, and a salad bar we opened at 11.00 in the morning because there really wasn't a market for our products earlier than that. We tried doughnuts and coffee and would do about $30 a day; not enough.

Biscuitville

I remember the exact time I thought of biscuits in our Pizzaville. I was on my way to our Chapel Hill Pizzaville, and it occurred to me that we could take the salad bar down at night and open the next morning with a jelly bar and freshly made buttermilk biscuits. I love sweets and could see people taking their biscuits down the line and getting all kinds of jams and jellies. So the next Pizzaville we opened (in High Point) we took the salad bar down at night and opened the next morning with a jelly bar. In addition to butter biscuits, we also had country ham and sausage biscuits. People would come in, look at the jelly bar and say, "Isn't that a cute idea? Give me a ham biscuit and a cup of coffee", and out the door they'd go. So we kept the biscuits and took the jelly bar out. I still have one of the jelly bar labels to remind me where we came from.

A restaurant chain called Chock-Full-O-Nuts "showed" me how we could cook country ham and sausage without a grill and hood system, which we did not have. They cooked hamburgers on a vertical grill that fried on one side and broiled on the other to lessen the need for a hood. However, they were prone to catch fire, and we eventually put in grill and hood systems. We put biscuits in all of our Pizzavilles. With the success of our biscuits, I wanted to try an all "biscuit" restaurant. Naturally, we would call it Biscuitville.

We opened our first Biscuitville in Danville, Virginia, in 1975 in an old Rich's Hamburgers building.

We served the same way we had served in a Pizzaville. We baked the biscuits in advance, loaded them plain or with ham and sausage and stored them in plastic containers. When we got the order we rang it up, turned around and put the biscuits in a small countertop pizza oven to reheat, got the beverages, took the warmed biscuits out of the oven, wrapped them, served them, and made the change. It was pretty efficient, and the biscuits were always warm.

Biscuitville

Later, we set up our Biscuitvilles with service similar to a
Wendy's, including the drive-through window. We baked the
biscuits on a conveyor oven as they were sold and held them
warm until we got the order. Then we assembled the biscuit
with just about anything you can think of that goes with a
biscuit: ham, sausage, cubed steak, fried chicken, cheese,
lettuce and tomato, etc. We also had platters with ham or
sausage, eggs, biscuits, and grits or any other side-order our
customers wanted. We have the freshest biscuits in the
industry.

One of the high points in our business was opening our
Biscuitville in North Asheboro. We opened there doing $12,000
a week, and that was big. What I should have done when we
opened Asheboro is to have dropped everything else and
concentrated on Biscuitville like we do now. Instead, like a true
entrepreneur I "tried" about a dozen different things. No use
listing them: the point is, when you stumble on something that
really works you should concentrate on that, almost single-
minded, like you're running in a straight line.

About that time I was able to get a high-school classmate,
Carrie Lasley, to come to work for us. Carrie went to secretarial
school after high school and had the biggest secretarial job in
Burlington as executive assistant to Joe Bird at Keyser-Roth. I

knew Joe pretty well and kept up with Carrie through him. He said not only was she the best assistant he could want, she was good to look at. So I knew she was good. She resigned from Keyser-Roth after her first child was born and I figured she would want to go back to work when both her children were in school. And she did. Carrie was a tremendous help to me for more than twenty years. She kept up with and remembered everything I couldn't.

Fran and Burney never worked much growing up. They asked me any number of times if they could get a job. I told them a lot of kids needed jobs and that at the time they did not; they should let the other kids get the jobs. I also told them that if we ever needed the income I would tell them, and they could get a job. When they went to work they would work long enough. Meanwhile, they both worked in the Biscuitvilles and The Cutting Board for enough time to see what it was like. I paid them both separately so it would not penalize the managers, who worked on profit share.

Burney runs the company now: second generation. He is already planning for possible third and fourth generation succession. Incidentally, Burney entered the business kind of through the back door. He started his own Spaghetti Bowl, but there was not enough demand in our area for a just spaghetti restaurant. So he closed it down and helped me find Biscuitville locations and then just worked his way into running the business.

As you can see, it took quite some time to go from flour salesman to bread store to pizza to biscuits. There is no substitute for the amount of personal time it takes to get a successful business started. But most businesses are not successful, no matter how much time a person puts in; most businesses fail. Income must exceed outgo or outgo must be less than income.

Later we converted all of our Pizzavilles to Biscuitvilles and concentrated on expanding Biscuitville. I used to go to all the restaurant conventions and exhibitions. I walked my feet right up to my knees looking for new or better equipment and new ideas. I did that for about five years. We still send people to shows and conventions.

Our Operators are compensated entirely on the performance of their Biscuitville store. At the beginning of the year they are assigned a percentage for their cost. Everything below that percentage is their "profit" share. In 2006–2007 our average Operator made almost $100,000 a year.

Accounting

About three months into our bread-store business, my
accountant said he was beginning to doubt the success of our
enterprise. With that, I cut costs to the bone. I was already
doing everything I could to increase sales. We reduced outgo to
less than income and went on from there. From the beginning
we have always had good accounting. I learned that from
McDonald's. I strongly believe if you are doing poorly, you want
to know why; if you are doing well you want to know why.

Real estate

Early on I looked for existing buildings, preferably existing
restaurant buildings. I have heard that an empty building is not
a good reason to go into business. However, I was doing the
best I could. Later, we built buildings from scratch; today we
build most of our buildings from scratch.

In the beginning I bought and paid for our equipment and
leased our land and buildings. That is conservative financing. I
should have been financing our equipment and buying and
financing our land and buildings. We would have made more
money. Many restaurant chains that have failed have been
saved from serious loss by their real estate values.

One day our Asheboro landlord called and asked me how long our initial lease was for. We usually got the initial part of our leases at a reduced price to see how the location would work. I said, "Two years." He said, "Right, but, that's not what the lease says." I said, "What does the lease say?" He said, "Ten years. What should we do?" I said, "We should do what we agreed on verbally." He said, "Good!" I said, "Would you give me another five-year option on the end?" He said he would. That's how we got along with our landlords.

Location is the most important decision you make in the restaurant business, and it's the hardest to change if you are wrong.

Sales

The key to the restaurant business is sales. High sales can cover up a lot of poor operating. Sales come from product mix, location, service, and price. Cleanliness is also important. Generally, people come to a restaurant because it has what they want and the food tastes good. People will put up with a lot of aggravation to get the food they want if it tastes like they want it to.

Recipes are important, but execution is also important. Consider this: the person in the seat in front of you has the recipe for Coca Cola in their pocket and you see it fall out on the floor in front of you. If you picked it up, do you think you would build another Coca Cola Company? Probably not.

Price is a big part of the quick-service business. However, it baffles me how some restaurants can regularly offer two-for-one. I feel like they know better than I what their product is worth. I have observed that when we raise prices we lose about an equal amount of volume, which does tend to lower our food costs, but we lose sales.

Advertising is important, and the best advertising is a good product.

I believe in magic in business. I believe some companies catch the public's fancy and get more sales because of it. Maybe quality, service, and cleanliness create magic.

I have been intrigued with "reported" average sales of restaurants. Some people's definition of average sales is the best week they ever had, projected. Also, I could not tell you how many different restaurants from the same company have been reported to have the highest sales in that company; makes you wonder.

We generally open at 6:00 a.m. and close at 2:00 p.m. That's more than one shift because somebody has to be at the store by 4:30 in the morning, and it takes at least an hour and a half after closing to clean up, do the accounting, and leave the building. That's at least eleven hours.

We have probably tried every combination of operating hours: 6:00 a.m. to 10:00 a.m. seven days a week, 6:00 a.m. to 10:00 a.m. closing on Mondays, 6:00 a.m. to 10:00 a.m. closing on Tuesdays 6:00 a.m. to 10:00 a.m. closing on Sundays; and 6:00 a.m. to 2:00 p.m. seven days a week. The latter is where we are today. We close half a day for Thanksgiving and all day on Christmas Day. It's easy for our customers to remember. A lot of people are on the move. Consequently, a lot of our food is consumed off premises.

People

We want our employees to be friendly, and I think they are. It starts from the top with our supervisors, our operators, and our line employees. Employees learn pretty quickly how we feel about customers, and they respond likewise. I was heading to a local restaurant in Burlington one day and said to myself, "Why am I going there? I'm not hungry. They don't have anything I want right now. Why am I going there? I'm going to see Johnny (Touloupus) at Zack's Hot Dogs. Because Johnny is so friendly." I strongly believe in training. Most employees want to do what you want them to do. They just don't know what it is you want them to do. We spend a lot of time and money on training. We made our first training films when we opened the first High Point Pizzaville. Two other employees and I would wait till they closed for the evening at 10:00 p.m. then move in and film until the morning crew came in at 4:30 a.m. It wasn't much fun, but it was productive.

Service, which goes along with friendliness, is another important part of the restaurant business. In our quick-service business, speed of service is very important. I sometimes walk out of quick-service restaurants if the service is too slow and the prospects of being served quickly are poor. Some of our customers probably do the same. However, if you see the line is moving, you're inclined to wait it out. Drive-through speed is the same.

People ask me if finding good labor isn't our biggest problem. I reply, "Labor is a big problem but our biggest problem is location. If we can find a good location we will find the people." We have found that where we have the hardest time finding help we do the most business. I have lost a lot of good people in the last forty years, and I have really been upset in some cases. But in one hundred per cent of the cases, within six months we had a better situation than before. Naturally, we try to keep our labor turnover as low as practicable. I didn't say as low as possible because some labor turnover is not all that bad. As I said, usually you end up with a better situation.

I always paid people as much as I possibly could. I was always more concerned about my labor cost than how much I paid people. I think we always paid more than the market, especially for managers. I think our Operators (Managers) are among the best paid in the industry, and I'm proud of that. We can do without a lot of people in our company, including me, but we cannot do without a manager at each restaurant.

In my opinion food and labor costs should be considered together. You can buy prepared food that costs more and take less time to get ready to sell. The food is more and the labor is less. It balances out. We want all of our employees to feel that they are part of our family, the Biscuitville family. If they have problems, we want to help. If they need something, we want to try to provide it.

Expenses
Expenses are a constant nickel-and-dime battle. Older buildings are more expensive to maintain.

Managing by walking around
There is no substitute for being in the restaurants, seeing things for yourself, and talking with the customers and employees. It is called *management by walking around*.

Aim

Aim is also important in our business. A friend once let me borrow a big restaurant chain's Operations Manual. After I read it, I said, "How in the world do they do all of that stuff?" He said, "They don't. But, if you aim here," and he raised his hand high, "... you may get here." He lowered his hand slightly. "And if you aim here," and he held his hand midways, "you will end up here." He lowered his hand.

Success

People ask me why we are successful. I reply, "Tenacity." I tell them we get up every morning and go at it. We keep on keeping on.

Luck

Most businessmen do not give enough credit to luck in their success. I think luck plays a big part in the success of any business. I know some people say the harder they work the luckier they are. That may be true, but I have seen a lot of people work hard and not be successful.

Health

I try to live healthy. Get plenty of sleep. Eat right. Don't smoke. Exercise five times a week. Walk on the treadmill for half an hour and workout with weights at the same time. Have regular physicals.

Personal money management

I believe that good personal money management may be one of the most important elements of good health and happiness. I call it "BS", Budget/Savings. The only thing I have seen that separates financially successful people from not so successful people is the ability to save money. Every truly successful person I have seen could save money. Either they made more money than they spent or they spent less money than they made.

I believe you should pay yourself first and save ten per cent of your income if possible. I do not believe in credit cards unless you can pay off the balance each and every month. I do not believe in credit card debt. I believe you should not buy anything on personal credit except your house.
I believe in education to help you get a better paying job.

Epilogue

Maurice Jennings is an unassuming man but one of considerable intelligence and business acumen who built his fledgling company into a major regional presence in the South. In one of Biscuitville's early TV campaigns it compared itself to the fictional "Circus Burger" where the biscuits were frozen, the "biscuit blocks" microwaved, and "eggs" as liquid as the summer rain flowing from a cardboard carton. At Biscuitville, however, there was "no fake food." The ad went on to position the chain's offerings as "Good Southern food fast. Without all the hoopla." Indeed. And that is how Biscuitville has so successfully built its business. At the core of its growth has been strategic positioning of its brand – without all the hoopla.

Chapter 4

The founder

The founder of a company is the North Star, the one who has universal significance to all serious students of business. Maurice Jennings founded Biscuitville in 1966. The 1970s were a lost decade for stocks. Maurice Jennings was part of a bumper crop of serious entrepreneurs bearing wagonloads of disruptive technologies. Southwest Airlines took off on its maiden flight in 1971. Microsoft, Apple, Oracle, Genentech, FedEx, and the SAS Institute in the Research Triangle Park in North Carolina all were started in that era.

The entrepreneurial breath of life was blown into the nostrils of the microprocessor. Critical development work on what would become the Internet was accomplished. The technologies of the time were so disruptive they were leap-frogging over the tall buildings housing mature industries and older technologies. Economist Joseph Schumpeter developed a new economic model to describe the 1970s, during which new disruptive technology destroyed the old.

Maurice had first shown signs of being a serial entrepreneur as a teenager. He founded Biscuitville without the benefit of family money. He had no outside investors. He did not use bank debt. Bootstrapping a start-up is every entrepreneur's dream come true. When growth is financed out of earnings, as in Biscuitville's case, there are no creditors or investors looking over your shoulders.

Between hyperinflation and the forty-nine per cent capital tax rate, there wasn't much risk capital available in the 1970s. Further adding to this bootstrap phenomenon was Maurice's entirely new quick-service business concept – to serve a great biscuit with the plan to do it faster and better than anybody else, so that when the "me-too's" showed up, he had already captured the high ground, becoming the classic first mover. As every businessperson knows, bootstrapping is non-dilutive. Having no stockholders to report to or banks needing to waive loan covenants saves time and untold emotional expense. Maurice accomplished his goals with his infectious sense of humor intact, noted senior manager John Huffman, hired by Jennings in 1975 when the second Biscuitville store opened in Martinsville, Virginia.

After Maurice Jennings returned state-side from the Air Force in 1955 to assist his father, who suffered a stroke that left him almost mute and marooned in a wheelchair, he moved from representing a bakery-ingredients company as a broker to running a bread shop, to owning a steak restaurant and ultimately to opening and successfully managing a pizza parlor, which Jennings finally morphed into the biscuit business.

Biscuitville is Maurice's masterpiece, his "Starry Night." This is not to deprecate his earlier successes, which were formidable, but Biscuitville is special. Jennings was the first to conceive and found a fast-food breakfast restaurant around the theme of grandma's golden homemade biscuits. Like its golden biscuits, the Golden Rule is fully part of the brand, integrating a top-selling product with an outstanding philosophy of employee loyalty, which Maurice used as the basis for extraordinary customer service.

Currently Chairman of the Board and an unofficial ambassador for the company, Jennings remains the heart and soul of the Biscuitville family.

Another Biscuitville Advisory Board member, William G. McNairy, marvels at Jennings' insight into the potential of others. Says McNairy, "Maurice saw the management potential of Darin Bailiff", who started with Biscuitville at the age of nineteen as a cook in store number 121 in 1978 and is now a District Supervisor and one of the highest paid employees in the company. Maurice saw a different fire in Darin as he cooked – the one in his belly. He no doubt recognized some of himself in the young man, and promoted him from cook to Assistant Manager, to Operator, and finally to District Supervisor. Darin is an effective and highly motivated manager. Maurice Jennings' genius is captured in Elbert Hubbard's quote: "There is something much more sacred, something finer by far, something rarer than ability. It is the ability to recognize ability." Maurice sees the ability and the fire within.

Another of Jennings' skills is the ability to fold when winning cards are elusive. CFO Jeff May says he learned one of his "key life's lessons" watching Jennings, who always recognized a good new money-making idea when he saw one and was never afraid to risk trying it. Conversely, once he saw the cards run against him, he would "fold" on the spot. CFO May admiringly took note of how quickly Founder Jennings made those decisions without a hint of bias toward even his own good or bad ideas.

Those who are privileged to know Maurice Jennings are amazed that a man who has achieved so much in his life can have such a deep sense of modesty, as evidenced by his philosophy about the role of luck in his success. His ability to form meaningful relationships across all cultural and income divides and his humility will be remembered as two of his greatest attributes.

Crawford Morgan is the operator of store number 132 in Greensboro, North Carolina. As a former employee of the Securities and Exchange Commission (SEC)-troubled Krispy Kreme, he was attracted to Biscuitville's high ethics. At Maurice Jennings' retirement party, Crawford noted how Maurice had left his distinct mark on Biscuitville and how each employee had a special place in their heart for him.

Maurice Jennings is a personality apart, but he is also a son of the South. Anyone who lives below the Mason–Dixon line knows there's something special about the South. Its charm lies not just in the beauty of blossoming crepe myrtles and azaleas and the smell of honeysuckle, but in its time-tested traditions and deeply ingrained values. Biscuitville has locations in North Carolina and Virginia and has a distinct Southern flavor.

W.J. Cash, speaking of the South in his watershed book, *The Mind of the South*, wrote in its introduction, "So far from being modernized, in many ways it has actually always marched away, as to this day it continues to do, from the present toward the past." Hence comes the charm often associated with this picturesque and often enigmatic region of the country.

The South is rich in tradition. Each year Augusta, Georgia, hosts that most genteel, enigmatic, and picturesque of all golf tournaments – the Masters. People drink sweet tea, sit in rocking chairs on front porches, stop in traffic to say "Hey!" to a friend, trust people simply because "my papa knows your papa", think of clogging as dancing and not something that stops up your drain, and, yes, eat those big, fluffy golden biscuits so endemic to the Southern lifestyle.

In *The Mind of the South*, Cash noted, "There exists among us a profound conviction that the South is another land, sharply differentiated from the rest of the American nation, and exhibiting within itself a remarkable homogeneity." This sentence was penned in 1940. In 2008, charming as it is, some of the uniqueness of the South has, unfortunately, eroded with time, but happily, not at Biscuitville.

For Maurice Jennings and Biscuitville employees, excellence is defined by being the best at producing that long-standing Southern tradition - the steaming hot golden breakfast biscuit. That biscuit is the secret to Biscuitville's success, and it's the best-kept secret in the country, even though it's clearly revealed on every one of Biscuitville's bags. Biscuitville was built around its delicious biscuit, and it is a proud heritage indeed! Everything Maurice Jennings did at Biscuitville was being done for the first time. He was and still is a true entrepreneurial visionary. Visionaries do not die; they do not fade away. Visionaries like Maurice remain in the corporate soul and in the hearts of the Biscuitville family, a family that stands on his broad shoulders.

With sheer grit, determination, and pluck, Maurice built the formidable brand that is Biscuitville.

Chapter 5

Branding
without all
the hoopla
"Fresh, friendly, fast"

Brand building is a misunderstood business concept. There is much chatter about branding, but little insight. By definition, branding is "the process of creating distinctive and durable perceptions in the minds of consumers."

A brand is "a persistent, unique business identity intertwined with associations of personality, quality, origin, liking and more." Branding, in the final analysis, is about connecting with the emotional "real estate" in the consumer's mind. It's about being memorable and creating a strong, visceral association between the product or service and the consumer.

To appreciate fully the importance of a brand is to understand that the substance of branding is affective. It operates in the catacombs below the line of visibility. To put this in perspective, trademarks or service marks, by comparison, are visible and readily identifiable, but the association is not as emotionally evocative. When American teenagers see an A&F logo on a pair of jeans, they know they were made by Abercrombie and Fitch. When they are watching TV and hear three chimes sound during a station break, most audiences identify the sound with the television network NBC. At the grocery store, if a large green man adorns the label of a vegetable can, consumers have been indoctrinated through commercials to recognize the Jolly Green Giant on that can of niblets corn. All of these are, by now, famous service marks or trademarks. They are seen and easily recognized by virtue of marketing.

There may or may not be a loyalty component to selecting one product or service over another. Teens may choose Aeropostale jeans over A&F jeans, or audiences may prefer Fox to NBC. On their way home, a working Mom or Dad may pick up the store brand over Green Giant. Changing fashion trends, on-going sales, a slow economic environment, personal preference, or any number of other factors guarantee that loyalty to particular products or services will ebb and flow and shift like sands in the desert. A trademark that's "hot" now may be cold six months from now, or have disappeared entirely. Still others have endured for a very long time.

Trademarks and service marks are more important in the life of a product than another marketing tool: patents. Patents, by definition, are a legally exclusive right to market a product for a pre-determined period of time. They have a finite life. The creative destruction of technology and the on-going discovery of new technology to take its place means the usable life of any given patent will probably be less than twenty years, since product development can have a two- to seven-year life cycle. Hence profit potential, or return on investment (ROI), for a patent's developer is limited.

In layman-speak, utility patents come and go, but trademarks are forever. Hence, return in investment on a trademark is of lengthier duration. A trademark has a useful life and generates profits for longer than a human lifespan. Levi Strauss, for example, is the oldest known apparel trademark in the US, having been protected by law since 1873. The oldest registered food trademark still in use in the United States is the red devil on cans of Underwood's deviled ham. It dates back to 1886. And perhaps the granddaddy of them all is Lowenbrau, whose founders contend for the oldest continuously used trademark in the world, claiming use since 1383. Now, that's one aged brewski!

Trademarks recommend themselves again when considering that the cost of obtaining a trademark is less than $3,000 compared to over $100,000 for a worldwide patent, excluding the costs of development, which are often enormous. When comparing investment in intellectual property versus brand, it is stunning how little capital is required to build a brand even considering the cost of searing brand identity into the minds of consumers.

What has all this to do with Biscuitville? Simply this: what other companies have achieved with intellectual property and patents, Biscuitville has accomplished by forging its formidable brand. Trademarks, with their infinite lives, are the vehicles by which companies bring their products to market. How successfully they have been able to implant that trademark – inculcate their brand into consumers minds – has been the difference between success and failure. But history has taught that intellectual capital is superior to profit gleaned from a commodities-based business. It is the most reliable way to wealth. Commodities can win in the short run but not over the long run.

Biscuitville wages battle daily for memorability in the consumer's mind against the dominant brands like Chick-fil-A, McDonald's, and Bojangles'. What insights allow Biscuitville to compete against these giants with their vast marketing firepower? How does Biscuitville achieve a high return on its branding investment?

Few plumb the subterranean catacombs of brand-building. It comes as no surprise that as a nation the U.S. is defined by consumerism; we are the most "shop-till-we-drop" society that has ever lived. Our susceptibility to marketing is enormous. It's all around us – broadcast and print media, billboards, the Internet, and it's spreading to even more unlikely venues. CBS Television announced recently that it will start etching ads for its new fall programming on about thirty-five million eggs! US Airways has found another use for the tray tables on its aircraft –advertisements. Among the companies plastering their ads on the backs of those tray tables are Verizon Wireless, GM, and Saab. In another show of advertising ingenuity, manholes in New York City are being covered with ads that look like a steaming cup of coffee. If only the odors the manholes emit would smell as good as their covers look!

In large part, we are ignorant of the power of branding. We choose to ignore it because it is so pervasive and, in many cases, darned annoying! Therefore, small businesses, in particular, that do not have access to or cannot afford to saturate the airwaves or advertise at the same level as their giant competitors, must conduct guerilla warfare to attract consumers' attention. Like the examples cited above, they must devise a unique way to get customers to focus on their message.

From its inception, Biscuitville began the process of differentiating itself from its competition. "Biscuitville" has been a registered trademark with the United States Patent and Trade Office since it began business in 1966. The company was the first Patent Office registrant to focus a quick-service business around a single product – the biscuit.

Establishing the "memorability" factor began with the biscuit but soon extended to the facades of the Biscuitville buildings. The golden yellow exteriors were constructed with the look and feel of old-time country homesteads and were distinctively identifiable, by design, as Biscuitville stores. Inside, the "down home" atmosphere evokes images of Grandmamma (or Mawmaw or Granny, depending upon which part of the South you're from) in her kitchen wielding a rolling pin over mounds of dough, taking the consumer's mind back to a simpler time and place when the kitchen was the focal point and gathering place in a home.

Biscuits are handmade in full view of customers, almost as if they were a part of the process, like Grandmamma's helpers in the kitchen. The atmosphere forms a powerful emotional bond with the consumer. It has been proven that the mind has a way of remembering pleasant times while filtering out many unpleasant memories. Key to developing a strong brand is building an emotional connection with those pleasant times in the mind of one's customers. This is particularly true in a time of anxiety, like the current recession, where warm and fuzzy is making a comeback, according to Stuart Elliot, writing in the *New York Times* of April 7, 2009. Biscuitville is warm and fuzzy, a brand folks feel comfortable with and can trust. At the same time, its brand is always relevant and never outdated. The biscuit is a staple in the South, even its own "food group," when made the Biscuitville way. The land grab is a fee simple claim to the emotional real estate of the mind, particularly if the emotion harkens back to pleasurable childhood remembrances in the loving, embracing bosom of your very own Grandmamma and the sights and smells of her homey, warm kitchen.

Memorability also means being the only choice for the consumer when deciding where to go for Sunday morning breakfast, or breakfast on any other day of the week for that matter. People want to go where they are known, loved, and treated with respect. Who doesn't gravitate to a business where they are greeted on a first-name basis? That's what Biscuitville strives to achieve. In addition to friendly, the service is also fast – very convenient when on your way to work. Employee turnover rates are one of the lowest in the industry. Chances are the person who greeted you today will be the same person who greets you a year from today. Try that at McDonald's!

The dignity of the person is respected at Biscuitville. Management views employees as family, and employees emulate management's behavior by treating their fellow employees in the same way. Maurice Jennings had a vision of a company that would serve only the freshest ingredients by the friendliest people. "Now forty-two years and fifty-three stores later, we are still standing true to his vision," said Kelli Hicks, Biscuitville's brand development and marketing director. "Thanks to our loyal customers and amazing team, we have enjoyed great success."

Biscuitville's "people-first" model of treating employees and customers with utmost care and respect means that customers, in turn, *are treated as employees treat one another*. They receive personal, top-quality service, another indelible mind impression in building distinctive brand identity.

Through a series of management and employee meetings and customer interviews, Biscuitville has also sought to educate and inspire its employees about Biscuitville's purpose and brand promise. "We wanted to share our history, who we are as a company, and our brand with our employees," says Hicks. All of Biscuitville's 941 employees were recently brand-certified over a four-week period, and the brand toolkit has been integrated into the company's induction program. "We did this program the right way," continued Hicks. "We took our time to work as a team to ensure its success, and we talked to our employees and got their buy in. We've already begun to look at ways to continually reinforce our brand promise of 'fresh, friendly, fast' to our employees and measure how well we are delivering it."

Brand would mean nothing without a high-quality product at a great value price. Biscuitville proudly promotes its Southern heritage: good Southern food. A "melt-the-real-estate-in-your-mind" biscuit and, says Hicks, "the freshness and quality of real eggs cracked and fried in front of you," is one of many ways Biscuitville competes with McDonald's boilerplate meal deals. But the psychographics are much more subtle and much more important. Customers still gravitate to the superior workmanship of food resulting in an original, made-from-scratch biscuit, despite the fact that McDonald's two-for-the-price-of-one deals are half Biscuitville's prices. Maurice Jennings has often said, "It baffles me how some restaurants can offer two for one regularly." And then, smiling wryly, adds, "I feel like they know better than I do what their product is worth." Biscuitville has consistently stood by its belief that quality, freshly made biscuits, and friendly service trump what its competition has to offer. Experience has shown that belief to be true. Biscuitville has built that "durable perception" of branding without massive advertising campaigns like those of Chick-fil-A, McDonald's or Bojangles'. It doesn't have to. In fact, Biscuitville is such a marketing contrarian that its competition must think its "low-fi" marketing is almost insulting.

Exploring the branding catacombs again in light of Biscuitville's approach, in a Biscuitville's customer's mind, he or she is down home with the Biscuitville way of life and doing business. The customer identifies with and is an extension of Biscuitville's soul. In *Positioning – the Battle of the Mind*, Reis and Trout use the French word *créneau* to describe the way the human mind can only capture the most important concept. For example, who was the second person to fly the Atlantic Ocean solo? How does Biscuitville capture that mind *créneau* in order to move breakfast customers into Biscuitville's camp and decline the giant breakfast fast-food competitors' fare? What is mind-capturing about the Biscuitville brand? In addition to the taste

advantage of the biscuit platform and all the quality foods
Biscuitville offers on that platform, the company has
substantial competitive advantages over all its competitors,
which significantly strengthen its brand's position in the
marketplace:

◆ Biscuitville's "people-first" program works. The Jenningses
  truly view employees as family. More importantly, employees
  quickly learn by example to treat all fellow employees with
  respect. This type of "benevolent humanism" extends to all
  employees, not just to bosses or their subordinates. The
  dignity of the person is celebrated at Biscuitville.

◆ The Biscuitville corollary is that customers, in turn, are
  treated as employees treat one another. Just like trademarks,
  service marks, logos, cleanliness, and community work, the
  behavior of employees as they connect to consumers is an
  integral part of branding.

◆ Biscuitville has earned the "buy-in" of its employees and has
  educated them on the importance of the Biscuitville brand
  to the success of the company.

◆ Inside each store is an entertaining and unique
  environment. The theatrical production of making biscuits
  from scratch in view of biscuit devotees provides the
  comfort of being in Grandmamma's kitchen.

◆ The delicious aroma of Southern cooking fills the air. People
  enjoy "hanging out" and engaging in small talk. Lingering

over these breakfasts in a warm, inviting atmosphere evokes memories of a wonderful simpler era gone by. For many, the atmosphere seals the deal. They'll be back again and again. The real estate of the mind is secure.

◆ The many archconservatives in the South know first hand about the cost of free lunches. If Biscuitville embraced the boilerplate meal deals, food quality would be the trade-off and would certainly suffer.

◆ Pricing is an integral part of Biscuitville's branding. Branding has lifted what Biscuitville sells out of the realm of a commodity, and its customers are willing to pay premium prices for premium products. Biscuitville has a brand that wins because its products resonate.

◆ The lean animal runs faster. Biscuitville is the original gazelle of the industry. A dearth of layers facilitates speed of communication from store level to John Huffman, Chief Operating Officer, Connie Bennett, Director of Operations, and the District Supervisors. This obviates lengthy approval processes for new initiatives, anything from store design to computer troubleshooting to new product introductions.

◆ Gold is both the symbol and the essence of this branding collage. It is no accident that the Biscuitville service mark and logo are colored gold. All fifty-three stores are gold. All of the 941 employees want to please and serve others. Certainly, Biscuitville has taken the golden biscuit and spun it into golden profits!

Biscuitville has etched its brand in the mindshare of an industry wrestling mightily to create brand awareness. The dominant brands continue to duke it out with international expansion, value menus, and Gatling gun-like advertising efforts. At the same time they struggle with low employee morale and high employee turnover in the face of new research evidencing the importance of meeting the psychological needs of employees.

High employee turnover – at nearly three hundred per cent industry-wide – is a huge contributor to poor service, especially because of the havoc it creates for training and employee retention initiatives. Poor service, in the long haul, torpedoes profits. It precludes the only sustainable competitive advantage in any business or industry: extraordinary service.

Contrast this with Biscuitville's one hundred and seventeen per cent employee turnover rate, one of the lowest in the industry. Consequently, the attention of competitors is diverted from food quality; "twofers", as they are known at Biscuitville, erode profits. Meanwhile, Biscuitville is laser-focused on its breakfast-only niche, continuing to stress extra-high-quality food and service, justifying premium prices.

Most importantly, Biscuitville, knowing where its biscuits are buttered, stays connected with its customers, never forgetting the values its founders first established. Over the years

Biscuitville

Biscuitville has become the only choice for biscuits to generations of Southerners who enjoy that trip down memory lane to Grandmamma's house "over yonder."

Biscuitville understands the consumer through and through, and its registered trademark, intellectual capital, and firmly entrenched brand is the key to its success. The way the company has positioned itself in its market and captured the hearts and minds of its customers has allowed it to identify and dominate a market niche. The economic value of market dominance, whether through identification with a trademark or through a branding "mind meld", to use a Vulcan euphemism, has been proven over and over.

Biscuitville has built an empire of good Southern food in the Southern regions it services. Its tactical strategy of capturing minds with its unique branding concept has been waged effectively and allowed it to capture a snippet of the minds of countless consumers served over the years.

Most importantly, once all costs are considered, Biscuitville has a near infinite return on investment on its trademark and the impeccable reputation of the brand attached to that mark. "Fresh biscuits. Friendly folks", without all the hoopla, has translated into a lot of "dough" for Biscuitville and will continue to do so for many profitable tomorrows.

Chapter 6

Ethics by example

By law, public companies must have written ethics policies. Such written policies are for the usual handful of employees who should not be on the payroll in the first place. The solution is to have a tough love discussion with the message, "I love you; I will miss you."

But the bigger problem is that a written policy is not panacea for ethics. The written policy does two things: it creates compliance and it raises the legal bar for the company. As the failure of parenthood in the old bromide has it: do as I say, not as I do.

Senior managers get their ethical cue from what top management does, not from a written ethics policy.

Raising the bar

Even though it makes the CEO feel mighty good to publish policy matters in writing, it gives attorneys the willies because it raises the price of poker. The ante goes up when policies are put in writing. Ethics statements, employee handbooks, and board committee charters should all be thought of as new laws the company must now abide by. Better to sit on your corporate hands than put in place written policies that even a handful of officers ignore. Even though a mission statement serves a useful purpose, never forget that people buy into the leader and their actions, not a written mission statement by itself.

Ethics

On Moral Duties (De Officiis) by Marcus Tullius Cicero is, without doubt, the greatest work on ethics ever written. He wrote *On Moral Duties* as a letter to educate his son, who sold his services to Augustus – Cicero's nemesis – and lent his name to the new order of Augustus. We now know books are not the panacea for ethics even if you have the advantage of kinship. You don't need another example of how great books themselves are no guide to the moral compass of right and wrong. That said, the story of theologian Dietrich Bonhoeffer's execution, at the hands of fellow Lutheran Judge Otto Thorbeck, just before the Third Reich fell, will weigh on any mind. Both Bonhoeffer and Thorbeck had received the same classical education, reading most of the same required books, yet Thorbeck carried out the trials he knew were wrong and sentenced Dietrich Bonhoeffer to be hanged by the German Gestapo on April 9, 1945.

What is ethical behavior?

Before determining the best way to imprint corporate ethics in the corporate soul, we must first ask, "What is ethical behavior?" Books, though useful in discussing ethics, are not the answer. Writings or postings in any form merely operate to raise the legal bar and give the writer a false sense of accomplishment.

Ethical behavior was in the teaching of Confucius when he first suggested that "doing unto others as you would have them do unto you" was practical advice for living. Five centuries later, this concept was validated by the Bible, and "loving God" added. Scholars have examined other attempts to define ethical behavior, including the current movement called WWJD (What would Jesus do?) that poses the spiritual and behavioral challenge of responding like Christ if faced with an ethical or moral dilemma. Alas, this might best define inadequacy instead.

But the "Golden Rule", as Confucius' and Jesus' radical definition of ethical behavior has come to be known, is true North. Other than a few bureaucrats, most would agree that written statements of ethics policy are not the solution; it is the actions of the leader; how she manifests herself in the circumstances. Written or oral statements of ethics are not bankable. Conduct is.

Biscuitville has no written ethics policy

Biscuitville has no written ethics policy. Like laws, policies dictate what can and cannot be done. Values inspire one's soul. It is a leader's job to inspire values in the workplace. Biscuitville's founder, Maurice Jennings, and CEO, Burney Jennings, live the sermon. It's about your conduct when no one other than God is looking. Both men, by the testimony of others, are ethical to the core. Both live ethically both as business leaders and in their personal lives. By all accounts, they try in every way to do to others as they expect will be done to them in return.

Maurice was a very visible CEO; Burney continues that visibility, which is so important in building a corporate family. He has continued his father's practice of MBWA – Management by Walking Around. Universally, people mimic the actions and conduct of others. Employees step into the footprints of the founder and CEO, the owners, and managers. Other employees, in turn, greatly influence even more employees when it comes to doing right by others.

It is unfortunate that public companies are lulled into compliance with the requirement of written ethics statements. Biscuitville has enviable bragging rights. The behavioral and ethical tone is set at the top, and ethical conduct throughout the organization is its witness. A written ethics policy is not necessary at Biscuitville. The sermon is lived, and all employees would have to be deaf, dumb, and blind not to get the message.

The greatest teachers, Jesus and Confucius among them, never put the Golden Rule in writing. The actions of these teachers were the lessons that changed lives and shaped the course of history.

The Biscuitville recipe for people

Biscuitville will always have an advantage over public companies as long as it counts human capital among its assets. During what will surely be seen as the "Great Recession of 2008–2012," marked by much distress, tumult, and uncertainty, Biscuitville's investment in people gives it moorings. More importantly, people equity will help gain market share during this turbulent time.

If human capital was appraised and recorded on the balance sheets, the boards of public companies would immediately begin asking hard questions about investments in human resources. Public company boards would suddenly value and recruit HR executives to serve on their boards rather than being almost exclusively populated with CEOs, former CEOs, and lawyers.

Questions about employee relations and welfare would suddenly appear on board agendas. Public company boards would cease announcing lay-offs and management bonuses at the same meetings!

If human capital were ever recorded and accounted for on financial statements, some companies would give it less weight than others. This would be based on false beliefs about what motivates people. Consider the following survey conducted by Chip Heath as part of his study, *Organizational Behavior and Human Decision Procedures*:

A $1,000 bonus is offered to employees if they meet certain performance targets. Most selected No.3 when asked which position would appeal to them personally:

1. Think of what that $1,000 means: a down payment on a new car or that new home improvement you've been wanting to make.

2. Think of the increased security of having $1,000 in your bank account for a rainy day.
3. Think of what the $1,000 means: the company recognizes how important you are to its overall performance. It doesn't spend money for nothing.

When asked which position would appeal to them personally, most selected Option 3. When asked which position would appeal to other people, most rank Option 1 followed by 3. The result shows that people are motivated by self-esteem, but falsely believe that others are motivated by money. Gaining self-esteem, learning, and self-actualization are greater motivators than money, after basic subsistence needs are met. That is why Biscuitville's "people first" philosophy has lifted the company to heights (and profits) other companies can only dream of.

Most have yet to understand the real importance of employee relations in building human capital and value to the stockholders. Biscuitville's Board of Advisors has long recognized the importance of investing in human capital and continuing to improve the process. Few public companies mention employee welfare, or have board agenda items addressing employee welfare. Biscuitville's Advisory Board minutes are heavy with references to employee morale and discussion of employee surveys.

Starting with Maurice and continuing with Burney, loyalty to all employees is a way of life. Management rightly believes talk is cheap; behavior is currency at Biscuitville. No one has to say, "We climb together;" all know that none will be left on the mountain to die. All Biscuitville managers have adopted and put into practice the example of the Jenningses.

Two families

During her twenty-four years with Biscuitville in multiple locations and with multiple management promotions to the level of District Supervisor over all the Eastern stores, Tonya Bullock tells of seeing John Huffman walking down the aisle at the funeral of her sister. Later, Tonya was diagnosed with breast cancer. She was told Biscuitville would stand by her fully, which turned out to mean she would be allowed to recover without any financial consequences whatsoever. Her discussion of her family and the Biscuitville family overlapped. It became apparent as she talked that she thought of them as one and the same. Certain stories stay in the mind forever. Many similar stories reverberate throughout Biscuitville. And everywhere it is impossible to get straight where the personal leaves off and the Biscuitville family begins.

Biscuitville, by practicing what it preaches, seems to have developed a living soul.

Chapter 7

The Golden Rule

And as ye would that men should do to you, do ye also to them likewise – **Luke 6:31**

Since the founding of Biscuitville in 1966, it has been a company mantra that all employees should be treated with respect. It is the way the early pioneers, Maurice Jennings and John Huffman, lived out their lives in front of the people beside whom they worked. Along with the golden biscuits came the Golden Rule, which, over the years, has become an integral part of the company's value system. Fairness and respect are not just words; they are a way of life at Biscuitville.

Biscuitville

The value of treating others as you would want to be treated was so central in the early days that employee welfare was more important than customer service. Normally in the land of capitalism, the customer is king. Employee welfare trails back in the far distance. How did and how does treating employees like family work so well at Biscuitville? How has it built such a loyal customer base?

Stories abound of unhappy employees who toil day after day at jobs they dislike, primarily for a paycheck. Going to work at Biscuitville is much more than a place to go to earn a bi-weekly bank deposit. Biscuitville is a nurturing place to work, where employees' psychological and social needs – belonging, acceptance, need for self-fulfillment, ability to learn new things, and opportunities for advancement – are carefully attended to by management. Employees are treated like people, and talent is recognized and encouraged.

The corporate hierarchy must establish rank, but equally respect must be given. Biscuitville employees are expected to treat their fellow employees with respect. No one at Biscuitville will tell you this is a hard thing to do. That's just how things are there. Amongst the co-workers of some companies in the public domain there is an utter lack of civility, sometimes bordering on abuse. Mutual respect was foundational in building what Maurice called the Biscuitville "family".

In turn, the Biscuitville customer is treated in the same way fellow employees treat one another. This is crucial. It explains why customer service at Biscuitville stores is superior in every way. Why are Biscuitville customers so loyal?

Uncompromisingly superior customer service, that's why! This has been confirmed repeatedly by customer service surveys, which are regularly carried out by management.

Another practice which distinguishes Biscuitville's concern for employee welfare from that of other companies is regular testing of the employee "waters", so to speak. When public company boards meet, their meetings rarely include an agenda item regarding human resource or employee concerns. In the rare instance when employee welfare is on the agenda, it appears last, when board members are pushing for adjournment to accommodate plane departure commitments. Jim Collins, in his best-selling book *Good to Great: Why Some Companies Make the Leap ... and Others Don't*, notes that great companies first decide who is going to be aboard the company bus before determining corporate mission and strategy. He asserts that the old adage "People are your most important asset" is wrong. He wisely amends this to say people are not your most important asset. The right people are.

Biscuitville

Dr. Isaac Horton, CEO of Remote Light, Inc., and the inventor
and holder of over 150 patents, has a unique viewpoint on the
debate over whether mission should continue to take
precedence over the right people. He notes, sadly, that world
businesses and especially corporate America continue to place
mission ahead of human relationships. A few firms place
mission and relationships as co-equal in importance. Dr. Horton
insists that both approaches are dead wrong and, agreeing
with Jim Collins, offers: "Relationships between and among
people trump mission and strategy." As an influential lay leader
and international speaker, he considers that even the churches
of our day are wrongheaded in placing emphasis on church
missions over relationships. After all, even Jesus, when
challenged to articulate the greatest of His commandments,
admonished that above all else we should first love the Lord
and then our neighbors as ourselves.

Biscuitville's advisory board agendas are all about the
Biscuitville family of employees. They intermittently include the
findings of employee satisfaction surveys. Problems, if any, are
addressed and resolved before small issues bubble into major
disruptions. Management knows the heartbeat of its
employees. Every pore of Biscuitville's culture oozes human
relationships first, mission second.

Biscuitville has other unique ways of building a close corporate family. Through forty-three years of operations the company has remained regional, with a distinct Southern heritage. Not only has heritage become an underpinning of the Biscuitville brand, but the band of Southern employees working at Biscuitville fosters closeness because of their shared backgrounds and history of Southern homogeneity. Though unfortunate in some circumstances, in Biscuitville's case, people gravitating toward others like themselves has created a bond among those who make up the Biscuitville team.

Chip Heath, now Professor of Organizational Behavior in the Stanford Graduate School of Business, conducted groundbreaking new research while he was a professor at Duke University's Fuqua School of Business. He concluded that Maslow's hierarchy of needs theory over-emphasized physiological needs, such as pay and safety, and under-emphasized the importance of psychological needs, such as self-fulfillment and learning new skills. Heath's study concludes that Maslow under-estimated the importance of an employee's social needs, such as esteem, self-actualization, and learning.

These findings reinforce Biscuitville's employee management model. Everyone at Biscuitville is a part of the "family", valued as a person, and contributes to the company's success. There is equal opportunity to learn, improve, be recognized for good work, help co-workers and the community, and move up in the ranks.

Admittedly, Biscuitville has benefited from good fortune and good timing in its business. Its long-standing emphasis on meeting the psychological and social needs of its employees, together with a singularly delicious biscuit made from the "secret" recipe Maurice put on and in the Biscuitville bags, have made Biscuitville an admired company, which, over the years, has attracted a cadre of talented and people-oriented employees.

The corporate world could benefit from the Biscuitville lesson of putting employees first, starting in the boardroom, where employee relations do not ordinarily rise to agenda level. This lesson will be difficult to put into practice because corporate America has spent decades treating employees with silent disdain.

Clearly, employee benevolence for forty-three years is a major reason why Biscuitville has attained what other companies sometimes never achieve - a sustainable competitive advantage.

Chapter 8

SCA
Sustainable competitive advantage

What exactly is a sustainable competitive advantage (SCA), why is it so important, and how has it contributed to Biscuitville's long-term success? 12manage, an online network on management methods, models, and concepts composed predominantly of senior managers who are decision-makers in major firms across the country, defines a sustainable competitive advantage as:

> The prolonged benefit of formulating and implementing some unique value-creating strategy not simultaneously being implemented by any current or potential competitors, along with the inability to duplicate or imitate the benefits of this strategy and the absence of threatening market developments.

Before a company has arrived at the point of having achieved such a *sustainable advantage*, it will have first accomplished excellence in one or more of the following areas: operational excellence, product leadership, and/or customer intimacy. What has made the advantage *sustainable* is the addition of one more crucial element: The company's "value creating things or capabilities ... cannot be duplicated or imitated by [its competitors], nor can they be made redundant by developments in the environment." In plain English, the company's product can't be easily imitated nor is there a readily available substitute for it in the marketplace. By this definition, beyond any shadow of a doubt, Biscuitville has achieved a sustainable competitive advantage in its industry. 12manage further states, "If a company makes a profit in excess of its cost of capital, it is probably able to do so because it has achieved a competitive position that offers some kind of edge over its current or potential rivals." That statement assumes a substantially lower financial matrix than Biscuitville's eye-catching year-on-year returns on investment, even without debt, which would further affect the number. Is a sustainable competitive advantage important? Absolutely! It is not only important, it is a strategic position to be coveted.

Which other companies have achieved an SCA, and how? Are there other niches in other industries that have achieved an

SCA similar to that of Biscuitville? The maestro of business, Warren Buffett, established the ultimate importance of SCA when he was asked what, in his experience, was the most important thing in evaluating a company. He replied, "sustainable competitive advantage." Ever a man willing to put his money where his belief is, he wrote billions of dollarsworth of checks to demonstrate his faith in SCA in building his hugely successful, multi-billion-dollar portfolio. Two examples of his major investments that demonstrate companies with an SCA:

◆ Coke – Coke's popular taste and trademark red and white containers are recognized even in the far reaches of the most remote places on the planet, like Mongolia and Timbuktu, which gives it its sustainable competitive advantage.

◆ Wal-Mart – Who hasn't heard of this global denizen of all things low-priced and plentiful? Wal-Mart, because of the economics of scale, is the de facto low-cost producer among popular retailers, bar none.

Community banks are an example of another industry that has achieved SCA by offering extraordinary customer service. Personal service, when coupled with a conservative balance sheet, could mean a bright future in the current economic environment for these small, more modest institutions, when compared with their larger brethren.

Biscuitville

Between 1992 and 2008 the number of US commercial banks
with under $100 million in assets shrank, the number dropping
by 5,410 (from over 8,000 to under 3,000 banks in that size
range). Large banks (with the top five banks accounting for
almost forty per cent of all deposits) had been able, until the
current US financial meltdown, to drive operational efficiencies
due to the economies of scale. The bigger banks had been the
low-cost producers, but the feeding frenzy for low-cost
mortgage loans left a mountain of toxic assets on their rotting
balance sheets. Who can forget all the big banks' CEOs
testifying before Congress and waiting in line like impoverished
children for a bailout?

A recent American Bankers Association survey on bank
marketing, conducted by Modalis Research, revealed that
seventy-three per cent of bank customers are willing to pay
more for service. Bank of America has been the low-cost
producer, but it is in financial difficulty and has been the
recipient of bailout funds from recent TARP (Troubled Asset
Relief Program) legislation. It is a large investment bank and is
not locally owned, not locally operated, and does not make
decisions on a local level like community bankers do.
Biscuitville is locally owned and locally managed by local
community members, who make decisions at the local level.
Community banks can say these same magic words. Even

though not low-cost producers, community bankers have prospered by providing personal service. At a community bank you can get access to the decision-makers and forge a relationship that may, and usually does, come in handy for many purposes. Customers are on a first-name basis with their banker, their kids go to school together, and they run into one another at church and the PTA. These personal relationships come in handy when a business loan is needed.

Community banks remain financially healthy in the midst of the bullet train of financial failures that have struck the big banks. The basic tenet of good service is to stay close to your customer like Biscuitville does.

Local ownership and service is also important to many other industries, including the hospitality industry. Dennis and Nancy King Quaintance and former Biscuitville advisory board member Mike Weaver have rebuilt the O. Henry Hotel, a Greensboro, North Carolina, neighbor of Biscuitville. Nancy and Dennis' concept for the hotel has been to bring back the neighborhood, community-centered, regal service of the original hotel built in 1919 by local business people. The original O. Henry Hotel was named after William Sidney Porter who wrote, under the famous pen-name O. Henry, famous works such as "The Gift of the Magi", "The Last Leaf" and "The Ransom of Red Chief". It brought to life the tradition of the community-centered, lavish, superb service hotels of the early 1900s. Today's rebuilt, lovingly restored, and passionately run O. Henry Hotel has brought back its neighborhood, and revived a lovely community landmark boasting royal service. The Proximity has been mentioned in *Southern Living* magazine, *Travel and Leisure* magazine, and promoted on the very popular *Today Show*, a national morning news show aired across the U.S.

Another recently built landmark hotel, The Proximity, boasts a five-star rating and has the distinction of being the "greenest" hotel in America. It is a LEED hotel, meaning it has met the standards of the Leadership in Energy and Environmental Design for environmentally-sustainable construction. For example, the building uses forty-one per cent less energy than a conventional hotel/restaurant by using ultra-efficient materials. The sun's energy heats hot water, with a hundred solar panels covering the four thousand square feet of rooftop (enough hot water for a hundred homes). This heats around sixty per cent of the water used in both the hotel and restaurant. Geothermal energy is used for the restaurant's refrigeration equipment, instead of a standard water-cooled system, saving significant amounts of water. Large, energy-efficient "operable" windows connect guests to the outdoors by providing a direct line of sight to the outdoor environment for more than ninety-seven per cent of all regularly occupied spaces. Building materials contain high levels of recycled materials. Eighty-seven per cent of construction waste was recycled, diverting 1,535 tons of debris from landfills. The Proximity was named one of the Top 50 New Business Hotels in the World by *Forbes* magazine, and it has already received the Automobile Association of America's prestigious Four Diamond Award.

The revitalized O. Henry Hotel and newly built Proximity are the pride of North Carolina's Piedmont Triad area. The personalized service and minute attention to detail have knighted both hotels with the same sword which dubbed the shoulders of Biscuitville.

Unlike large banks, which recently have failed on a massive scale, some companies continue to employ with good success the strategy of being the low-cost producer in their industry. Michael Porter, leader of the Institute for Strategy and Competitiveness at Harvard University, studies competition and its implications for company strategy. He says that many companies like Timex, for example, may set out to become a low-cost producer in their industry, achieving economies of scale, which becomes a competitive advantage. Timex produces low-cost, affordable watches for broad distribution through many retail outlets.

Another competitive strategy, notes Porter, is differentiation. Another watchmaker, like Rolex, may distinguish itself from a company like Timex that might otherwise have become its direct competition, and achieve a sustainable competitive advantage by cultivating a particular image in its industry and producing high-end, exquisite gold watches for upscale consumers. Each watchmaker, by using strategies of low-cost production and differentiation achieves its own SCA within the same industry.

Intel, the computer chipmaker, has set itself apart from other chipmakers in the highly competitive computer industry. SCA is figuratively emblazoned upon its income statements by means of differentiation. Intel's ability to design and manufacture ever more powerful microprocessors for PCs has fueled its SCA. Intel meets Buffett's investment criteria. But, alas, he passes on all investment opportunities when he does not understand the underlying business.

Why don't patents, the equivalent of a legal twenty-year monopoly, give rise to an SCA? Why are technology companies, when awarded patents, not elevated to the top spot on the Olympic podium and bestowed a ribbon with a coveted SCA gold medal? Sustainability is not measured in calendar time. Nor does sustainability mean that the advantage will last forever. In the business literature, sustainability suggests that the advantage lasts long enough for competitors to stop trying to duplicate the strategy that gave rise to their competitor's SCA.

As a result, micro-electrics and biotechnology modalities and products subject to patent expiration do not rise to the level of sustainability. First, the patent life is only twenty years. More importantly, the sustainable advantage of a patent is typically leap-frogged by new waves of better technology, development of new chemical compounds, and advances in sciences subject to patents. Unlike a patent, a trademark is the gold standard – forever and a day. Registered trademarks, like Coke and Biscuitville, give rise to a sustainable competitive advantage.

The Biscuitville trademark is on an upward trajectory, as was discussed at length in chapter 5. Biscuitville's trademark has not yet achieved the SCA status of Coke. But the company has achieved a sustainable competitive advantage on multiple levels by employing many of the strategies discussed above. How did Biscuitville achieve a competency that cannot be easily pursued by its competitors? Maurice Jennings' first step was to understand that human relationships trump an articulated corporate mission. Worry first about who is going to have a seat on the company bus. Cement those relationships.

Invest time and money in employees. Do just like your mama taught you, and form ethical standards for how you live each and every day. Even though relationships are not accounted for in the profit and loss account, cash flow, or balance sheet, understanding and encouraging people skills and working together as a team are the essence of Biscuitville's success. As technology continues to advance, human touch becomes even more important. High tech, high touch. The finishing stroke is to insist, yes, demand that all employees, regardless of rank, treat each other equally and with equal respect, and work together for the good of all.

Biscuitville has accomplished much of its SCA by building relationships with all 941 of its employees. Previously, the importance of extraordinary service predicated on close relationships among employees was not well understood nor appreciated as a way to achieve a sustainable competitive advantage. Here Biscuitville's story is instructive. The company's "people-first" culture has translated to superior customer service.

Extraordinary service is the ultimate sustainable competitive advantage. Add to the latter superior products, exceptional profitability, and dominance in its market, and Biscuitville is unrivaled in its industry and within its marketing footprint. Biscuitville could well be the new definition of sustainable competitive advantage.

Chapter 9

Chief crank-turner

A first visit with Maurice Jennings leaves you with the feeling that he has been your life-long buddy. It is easy, in his company, to hearken back to an era when life was less complicated and more laid back. Visions of him rowing a flat-bottomed boat over a cool sparkling pond on a hot, hazy summer afternoon come to mind. He is comfortable in his skin, and there's a quality about him that makes you feel just as comfortable in your own.

Even in his humility, though, you intuitively sense an inner strength about him, one that instantly makes you recognize that you are in the presence a man of vision, someone fascinated by the possibilities, interested in the broad strokes, a person who has gravitated directly past the snapshots to the cyclorama itself – a man of hard work and steely determination despite his easy-going exterior.

Biscuitville

The history of Biscuitville confirms that intuition. Using achievement of non-financial milestones, Maurice was without peer in devising and implementing the model for his young start-up company. More impressively, he grew Biscuitville without the financial assistance of outside investors. Biscuitville never required a bank loan to fund its growth. This is remarkable for any company but particularly so for one experiencing rapid growth.

The pace of Biscuitville's growth required a significant permanent investment in net working capital. Its ultimate expansion to 941 employees was entirely financed by internal cash flow: EBITDA (earnings before interest, taxes, depreciation, and amortization) with a giant "E"! To its credit, Biscuitville never relied on OPM – other people's money – to make it a successful enterprise; a financially and emotionally satisfying feat for Maurice.

As in all start-ups, the measure of success cannot be just margins and return on investment: that comes later. Rather, achieving milestones of revenue growth and persuading employees, vendors, and other key venture partners that the business model makes logical sense are critical, as are being temperate in dealing with the risks inherent in surviving day-to-day in swift and unpredictable economic rapids. It has

frequently been noted as America takes inventory of its place in history that its most powerful economic strength is its appetite for entrepreneurial risk. Maurice, a fearless sort, excelled as an entrepreneur. He surrounded himself with a superior group of employees, all professionals who complemented his prescience. This was the original vision Maurice was to pass on to his son, Maurice Neuborne Jennings, Jr., known fondly within the company as "Burney."
Other than sharing both his father's Christian ideals and surname and the family's deep, abiding commitment to the welfare of the Biscuitville employee family, Burney – the next generation – is very much his own person.

In January 1987 he graduated from Elon University, where he is now a Trustee like his father before him. Burney was a serious student, according to Dr. Martin L. Schotzberger, who recalls that during his time on campus Burney was inseparable from another student named Dina Blake, whom he has known since childhood. The relationship would lead to matrimony. Dina became Burney's first and only wife on December 27, 1986 and is the mother of their four children – Blake, 20, Bailey, 18, Mary Frances, 16, and John, 14.

After college, Maurice neither encouraged nor discouraged Burney from following in his footsteps by working for Biscuitville. However, Maurice wisely advised Burney that if he did join the company, he would have to earn his stripes just like all management had done. He would have to climb his way up the ladder the old-fashioned way – hard work at each step, plus a good bit of pluck. Burney signed on.

In his own words, Burney says, "I worked various positions ... I looked for locations, then opened the Spaghetti Bowl and then was responsible for the Cutting Board as President. Then I became the Biscuitville CFO and was responsible for real estate." Real estate entailed selecting new sites for stores as the company expanded its business sphere. In site selection for quick-service restaurants there are three rules – location, location, location – and the first three count the most! Picking sites is absolutely critical in all industries, but it is life and death in the early days of a quick-service business. Successful site selection is telegraphed immediately. As in the Roman Coliseum, it's either thumbs up or thumbs down. Life or death is decided quickly. A company lives or dies by where it places its stores. Fortunately, Burney did not disappoint at this task.

As CFO, Burney was equally adept at managing Biscuitville's financial matters. The decisions of a CFO are almost immediately apparent and measurable, allowing for quick and unambiguous feedback to all senior managers. Maurice's grooming of his son was, in effect, a rigorous and robust CEO succession plan. Maurice, wisely, greatly minimized the risks of succession strategy by observing his son in important roles within Biscuitville before making the ultimate decision to place him in a position of greater importance, namely that of CEO. The failure rate of recruiting an outside CEO is substantially greater than hiring from within the company. It would have been a huge risk for Maurice to look for an outside candidate as his eventual successor. But Burney's aptitude obviated this risk. He proved his mettle. Burney earned the right to be "Chief Crank-Turner (CCT)."

Burney Jennings was elevated to Company President in 1996 and to CEO in 1999. During Burney's scrupulous training, Biscuitville was crossing the chasm from early adopter to the consumer mass market essential to the commercialization of any enterprise. The importance of that transformation, and the drama inherent in Biscuitville's rapid new cycle of growth, were palpable.

Burney took the helm of Biscuitville during a strategic inflection point where fundamentals were changing from an emerging to a mature company undergoing rapid growth. His challenge was to take Biscuitville to the next level of growth and profits with an emphasis on plan, budget, accountability, and execution. Again, Burney excelled by focusing on Biscuitville's internal health, emphasizing especially employee self-esteem as a contributor to profitability.

Just how successful has Burney Jennings been as CEO/CCT since he ascended to the helm of Biscuitville? By what standard is a CEO to be measured? The CEO is unequivocally charged with the duty to make money for the shareholders. Unlike milestones used in assessing the performance of a start-up, return on investment is universally recognized as the measuring stick by which all CEOs are evaluated when any company has been commercialized. ROI is a metric indicating whether or not a firm is using its resources in an efficient manner, and has traditionally been closely linked to CEO performance.

ROI for a particular accounting period is a measure of the benefit (return) of an investment divided by the cost of the investment; the result is expressed as a percentage. Using that measure, Burney Jennings is a crank-turner at the top of the top quartile of CEOs. Over the last five years, Biscuitville's ROI compares favorably with the upper crust of the *Fortune* 100 companies, ranked only behind Dell and in a virtual tie with Verizon, both high-tech companies.

What singular traits differentiate those select few highly accomplished CEOs from other, less notable CEOs and set them apart as superior managers? What distinguishes Burney Jennings from and makes him unique among his peers? Aside from his astonishing numbers, he doesn't "look" the part. He would never be mistaken for an investment banker. There is nothing stiff or staid about the man. His dress is anything but "pinstripe." Casual is the order of most of Burney's days.

Though his demeanor is reserved, Burney also doesn't act the part of the stereotypical aloof, distant, unapproachable, "hidden in his office" manager. Most fortunately, he has never aspired to be among the acclaimed charismatic CEOs of the last decade who so famously – and infamously – drove their *Fortune* 500 companies into highly public, embarrassing bankruptcies, never to be heard of again, except as the brunt of bad jokes and ridicule. Professor Rakesh Khurana, Professor of Business Administration at Harvard Business School, has cautioned against what he refers to as the "irrational search for charismatic CEOs", calling such an endeavor "a misguided belief that a CEO with a magnetic personality translates to corporate success (it doesn't)." Burney and others like him have shone a bright light on the importance of crank-turning CEOs who deliver results, not promises. Charisma, at Biscuitville, takes a back seat to tending to the shareholders' business and serving customers by ensuring that the company's actual results are in line with what it had budgeted for the year.

Biscuitville

The way of governing at Biscuitville has traditionally been, as Maurice once observed, "Management by Walking Around" (MBWA). Just what is MBWA? Burney visits each of the fifty-one stores twice annually. During one such visit, a store had gotten into a crunch. Burney jumped into the fray and started fixing drinks at the drive-through window, enjoying, as Andy Warhol once quipped, his fifteen minutes of fame!

In continuing that long-standing tradition, Burney has had much deliberate interaction with his employees. MBWA has proven to be a useful tool for providing management with meaningful, first-hand input from field operations. However, the real value is to the employees. It affirms their self-worth to have a CEO who takes the time personally to visit their shops and speak to each of them directly, and who cares about what they have to say. They understand that a personal relationship means greater job security and a lesser likelihood that a lay-off or change in their status would be undertaken without first exhausting every alternative for their benefit.

Burney is a good listener. Those who study such things have concluded that listening with the mind and absorbing what is said is a true act of love. In *Listening Is an Act of Love*, acclaimed radio producer Dave Isay records forty-nine excerpts from the 10,000 interviews people have recorded from StoryCorps, the largest and most ambitious private oral history project in American history. (The series can also be heard on NPR radio stations throughout the US.) Recording booths were made available around the nation – in New York City at two permanent booths (at Grand Central Station and Ground Zero) and in one of the three mobile booths touring the country – since the project's launch four years ago. Isay says, "I realized how many people among us feel completely invisible, believe their lives don't matter, and fear they'll someday be forgotten." As simple stories of humanity, each StoryCorps tale has its own potency, with themes of family, love, dedication, and struggle. This is the kind of sincere connection Maurice and now Burney have endeavored to cultivate with their Biscuitville "family". MBWA and sincere listening makes that possible. Unlike bankers, imperial corporate types, and some in government who seem to have the unfortunate reputation of knowing everything and listening to no one, Burney pays close attention to what he is told. Biscuitville folks refer to their family and Biscuitville employees in the same breath. This is confusing until you realize this is just the way conversations go at Biscuitville.

Burney emphatically shares the belief of "people first" in the same profound way as his father, which is key to any relationship with line and staff employees as well as managers up the ladder of accountability. It means walking in someone else's shoes and sharing the universal elements of another person's struggle, connecting with some quality in them that finds its counterpart in one's own private world. That's the Biscuitville "Way".

MBWA may very well be Biscuitville's financial "Secret Garden". Happy employees equal profits. Burney also fully shares Maurice's emphasis on investing in professional improvement and development of employees. He also places high importance on his employees' knowledge of the Biscuitville brand, the company's vision, and plans for future growth. Company seminars educate employees and allow them to educate each other on branding and its relationship to customer loyalty and impact on the bottom line.

Burney takes the temperature of his company on his secret garden visits as well as by intuitive wisdom. These are uncommon traits in a CEO, which have proven invaluable in perpetuating a corporate culture of success built on a firm foundation of "people first." Burney is that rarest of CEOs in today's corporate America, one who understands that the first and most important resource is the human resource. Take care of your people, and the "dough" will rise nicely.

What does it take to earn the moniker CCT – Chief Crank-Turner? The answer is to be the consummate manager. Burney is that and more. He develops and implements corporate goals, especially the proximate goals, and sets out to achieve them. He insists upon accountability. Actual versus budget figures receive close scrutiny. More deliberate than his venturesome and fearless father, Burney achieves big goals by taking measured steps. As he takes those deliberate steps, he measures others' progress and seeks accountability.

Burney also adapts to changing conditions. Biscuitville is not the same company it was in Maurice's day. It is growing steadily and has had to acclimatize to changing technologies, increased competition, heightened interface with governments and agencies, and challenging economic conditions. Nevertheless, Biscuitville continues its steady and consistent growth while others in its industry have failed or their fortunes have fallen to extreme economic pressures or poor management.

Former Treasury Secretary Hank Paulson famously said, "I've always said to everyone that ever worked for me, if you get too dug in on a position, the facts change, and if you don't change to adapt to the facts, you will never be successful." Burney has practiced this philosophy during his tenure as CEO and was a classic over-achiever in all his jobs leading up to and earning the position of CEO and the mightiest title, CCT.

People are more consistent than not, but it took lengthy visits with Burney, Jeff May, John Huffman, and numerous Biscuitville employees to identify what is perhaps Burney's most outstanding personal trait: consistency of character. He speaks for himself and his company with one voice. We believe we know someone; we know what to expect, or, we think we do. There is that certain annoying someone who has mood swings without cause or that other whose personality goes from hot to cold. There is nothing in the workplace more disconcerting than inconsistency. But not with Burney. He is the epitome of character consistency. His calm, steady demeanor provides an emotional template for the workplace and enhances his ability to motivate and build an effective, cohesive team.

While Maurice was Captain Courageous, Burney, as Chief Executive Officer of Biscuitville, is all about soft power. Today, from CEOs to drill sergeants, the emphasis is less on barking orders and more on eliciting participation. That is Burney's management style. Yet he is firmly in control. In leadership circles and in Burney's sphere, soft power is on the rise. Maurice and Burney have worked cooperatively to make Biscuitville the company it is today. Historical and fictional literature is replete with father–son dysfunctional relationships: Absalom, the third son of King David, rebelled against him, and eventually met his death when his long hair got caught in a tree as he was fleeing in his chariot; in Sophocles' play, Oedipus fulfilled a prophecy that he would kill his father, Laius; Sir Mordred's mortal combat with his father, King Arthur resulted in the demise of idyllic Camelot. No such bitter dysfunction exists between Maurice and Burney. Though the measure of success for each generation of Jennings leadership of Biscuitville is unique and distinct, first and foremost the relationship between father and son is built on abiding love and mutual respect.

The relationship of love and trust between a father and son is not a given in life or in fiction. Thus, the close relationship between Maurice and Burney is to be celebrated. It has been critical and absolutely key to the strength and success of the company over one-third of a century. In fact, Burney's succession to the helm at Biscuitville would have been impossible without it.

The two Jenningses' dichotomous leadership styles at Biscuitville have turned out to be fortuitous. Maurice, the leadoff hitter, was a serial entrepreneur. Burney, the clean-up hitter, hit singles to drive in runs. Actual versus budget is all about runs batted in too. Together, they are a formidable team. Of course, no company can be successful without considerable business acumen. Both Maurice and Burney are gifted businessmen. As any company moves from start-up to emerging company to finally crossing the chasm to commercialization and maturation, different executive skill sets are needed. Maurice is an entrepreneurial risk-taker in the American tradition, with a demonstrated ability to make alpha decisions on the fly. Burney is the man who now keeps Maurice's ship on an even keel and has done so with great aplomb through some very difficult economic storms.

Maurice's vision and entrepreneurship breathed life into the nascent Biscuitville in 1966. Burney has nurtured Biscuitville's heart and soul. The living thriving entity that is Biscuitville today has been lucky to have a serial entrepreneur and visionary as the founder, followed by his son, the consummate transactional manager and supreme crank-turner.

Together Maurice and Burney Jennings have built Biscuitville into a commercial powerhouse where the "dough" not only turns into a delicious biscuit but also turns a highly bankable shade of green. Biscuitville customers will always be able to depend on the fact that the product is what it claims to be – high quality and fresh - every time they carry away an egg and cheese biscuit in one of Biscuitville's little brown bags.

Chapter 10

It's in the bag

Every good Southern boy and girl is well acquainted with the motherly send-off, "Remember who you are!" These words followed us out the door every time we left home, whether we were leaving for five minutes or five years. Our mothers and grandmothers dished this benevolent admonition from a deep well of wisdom throughout our growing up years. If only they had been there to remind every individual, group, race, and nation throughout the ages, we could have stopped praying for Kingdom Come years ago.

For a clear example of what it means to "remember who you are," one need look no further than Biscuitville. In fact, not only do they remember who they are, they also make sure you don't forget either!

Biscuitville

Biscuitville's vision of who they are imbues their modus operandi with an elegant simplicity of purpose. In fact, Biscuitville may well be the only company anywhere to put its desiderata right on its bags, which are mini-ads telling you of the company's longevity, and a continual reminder of why people keep coming back, as if the smell and the taste of the best fresh homemade egg and cheese biscuits in the South weren't reminder enough.

It only takes a couple of minutes for a newbie to Biscuitville to fall head-over-heels in love with the down-home quality of a Biscuitville store and the melodious sound of a friendly Southern accent drawling charmingly, "How can I help you?" Translation: "How can I make your day better than when you walked in the door?" The wonderful smell of grandmamma's homemade biscuits wafts from the serving window where a to-die-for fresh egg and cheese biscuit is made, wrapped and handed to you in an otherwise ordinary-looking brown-paper bag, the kind any Mom would send to school with her six year-old first-grader, except that this bag has a gold star emblazoned across the front, informing the bearer that Biscuitville has been around since 1966. Pretty remarkable for a small, private, family-owned company that has since blossomed into an extraordinary little giant in its industry.

The bag continues to reveal more secrets. At the top of one side is Biscuitville's registered service mark – a rolling pin, identical to one grandmamma might have used in her kitchen when you were little. Underneath the rolling pin, a caption tells its family of customers that Biscuitville's identity is *"fresh biscuits, friendly folks."* But you knew that already. You were just inside, and now you're chowing down that hot egg and cheese delight you just purchased. You probably won't need reminding, but the company wants to let you know just the same.

While you're enjoying all that golden goodness you might turn the bag over and notice that on the other side it says you are the happy recipient of not just fresh food, but "the freshest food" and not just quality ingredients but "the highest quality ingredients." Your biscuit is exceptionally tasty, it's made of the highest quality ingredients, and it was made homemade fresh – just for you.

For those who want to learn more about the company, Biscuitville places its web address – www.biscuitville.com – on the bottom of the bag.

You now know all of the company's secrets. In essence, the bag and the biscuits inside are a metaphor for the company itself. They tell customers all they need to know about the company's customer service, ethics, philosophy, and product quality – the freshest food, the highest quality ingredients, delivered with fast, friendly customer service.

It's in the bag!

Chapter 11

Soft power, hard dollars

In the first third of the twentieth century, it would not be an oversimplification to say that labor was both abundant and abused. During the second third, labor gained the wages and respect that it rightly deserved. The last third of the century saw labor lose its way, particularly as jobs moved offshore as a result of cheaper labor costs in third-world countries. On the other end of the fulcrum, management was lifted up. It gained prominence as labor costs declined. This mega-trend continued as CEOs began wielding the scepter of imperialism.

The general rise of the management class in the latter third of the twentieth century profoundly changed management as a profession. The history of Biscuitville, founded in 1966, has been impacted by these management changes. The generation that came home after the Second World War, known as the Great

Generation, managed in a structural hierarchy identically to the military they had led. *The Man In the Grey Flannel Suit*, by Sloan Wilson, was a seminal book detailing management style and practices. It examines the life of Tom Rath, a businessman forced to conform to stodgy and strict business practices imposed by his managers in order to get ahead but who, in the end, chooses a less stressful job in order to bring more balance into his personal life. Sociologists have often cited the book with reference to America's discontented businessmen. Maurice Jennings served with distinction in the military. Even though he was of the "Command and Control" generation, he opted neither for the pinstripe suit nor the bureaucracy. His entrepreneurial bent was so strong that he founded several successful food enterprises. Biscuitville was his last, and, like an accomplished artistic endeavor, it turned out to be his "Starry Night."

During Biscuitville's founding years, Maurice's belief in his company, his attention to its growth, and his management practices gave him all the outward trappings of a charismatic imperial CEO. He came to have something akin to rock star quality. But Maurice was certainly not imperialistic, even though his leadership had grown Biscuitville to four hundred employees by the 1980s, which would have qualified him to count himself among the new imperial CEO breed which was in place in the last two decades of the twentieth century. But that's not who he was as a person or a leader. Maurice had no interest in assuming an imperial CEO's throne. He did not even want a private parking space, although he frequently got prime parking by being the earliest to work. Though Maurice's management style was transformational versus Burney's transactional approach, neither man's style could ever be described as imperial. That would require a level of arrogance neither has ever possessed.

Burney Jennings assumed the CEO title in 1996. Even though few realized it at the time, in hindsight, by the time Burney assumed the helm, the definition of effective leadership was beginning to move away from imperial CEO command-and-control style of leadership to participatory management. Enron and Worldcom would then come along to drive the nails into the imperial CEO coffin. But at Biscuitville, participatory management was a style ready made for Burney.

Some describe participatory management in terms of servant leadership. A major contributor to the rise of the concept of participatory management was the availability of the Internet. Suddenly, many more at the bottom and middle layers of the corporate hierarchy gained information at or near the same time as senior management. Technology-savvy junior management always had information before top management, but as more Web users became Internet savvy, a wealth of information was a mere keystroke away. Executives were no longer the only subset privy to even the most sensitive information, thereby forcing management to become more open.

Burney's management style is and has always been participatory. He carries no scepter of charisma in an industry replete with pitchmen-in-chief like Ray Kroc of McDonald's and Truett Cathy of Chick-fil-A. He is a breath of fresh air among managers, a man well before his time who actively solicits advice from others. He is certainly more servant leader than commander and controller. The best way to characterize his management style is "soft power."

Soft power is a term coined by Joseph S. Nye, Jr., in *The Powers to Lead*. Nye writes, "Instead of just shaping others to their wills, leaders have to attract support by also shaping themselves to their followers." As the hierarchies within corporations have become more ill-defined because of the widespread use of the Internet and the plethora of information now available on the World Wide Web, leadership has, of necessity, been diluted. From CEOs to Marine drill sergeants, the emphasis is less on giving commands and controlling others. The order of the day is eliciting participation.

At the same time, however, Burney Jennings is no less a CEO, nor does he wield less power than that office requires. He would agree with *Fortune* magazine's senior editor Alex Taylor III, who recently demonstrated that over time General Motor's top executives have lost the ability to execute, resulting in CEO Rick Wagner's trapdoor exit. Burney has not. Plan versus actual and accountability are elements of soft power, yet remain essential and vital to Biscuitville's bottom line.

Though he believes in the Japanese proverb, "None of us is as smart as all of us", soft power in Burney's hands is, nonetheless, extremely powerful. He has the ability to use what he learns by working with his managers and employees as a close-knit, one-for-all and all-for-one team and translating it into profits. Burney Jennings practices this new soft power to produce hard dollars for the shareholders of Biscuitville.

Chapter 12

A best company to work for

Fortune magazine publishes an annual list of the 100 Best Companies to Work For® in the United States. This list is made up primarily, although not exclusively, of public companies with a thousand or more employees. Biscuitville could be considered for the list for the first time in 2010.

The current one hundred companies on *Fortune's* list are noteworthy because, like Biscuitville, they are employee-friendly, shun lay-offs, embrace diversity, and offer perks and benefits that inspire employees to "buy in" to the company culture and stick around longer, rather than move from job to job. Biscuitville has never had a company-wide or mass employee lay-off in its history and hopes it can still make that claim when it celebrates having been in business for a half-century in 2016.

Biscuitville

The company cultures, management philosophies, and respect for employees adopted by the companies in the *Fortune* 100 lists in 2008 and 2009 make them such attractive places to work. Biscuitville mirrors their ethos. Here's a sample:

◆ Net App jumped to the top spot in 2009 with its legendary egalitarian culture. One employee commented that Net App feels like "a small startup company instead of a 7,000-plus corporation." Says *Fortune*, "Typical of its down-to-earth management ethos, Net App early on ditched a travel policy a dozen pages long in favor of the maxim: "We are a frugal company. But don't show up dog-tired to save a few bucks. Use common sense."

◆ QuikTrip is a twenty-four-hour convenience store chain with employees who are treated so well in terms of wages, benefits, and training that *Fortune* says that workers stay around for the "long haul." More than two hundred have been with the company for over twenty years, a rarity in today's mobile job market.

◆ Nugget Market, described by *Fortune* as a "crazy-fun supermarket chain" made the list for never having had a lay-off in its eighty-one-year long history.

◆ Shared Technologies, an installer of data and telephone systems, hit what *Fortune* described as a "slow patch" in 2008. As a result, "senior managers gave up bonuses, CEO Tony Parella cut his salary by fifty per cent, travel costs were reduced, and open positions were left unfilled. Result: Not a single lay-off." Parella visits all forty-one locations to talk to his workers. Says one employee of his CEO, "I'd follow Tony off a bridge."

◆ SAS moved up *Fortune's* ratings from the twenty-ninth in 2007 to twentieth in 2008. There have been no lay-offs at this leading supplier of software located in the Research Triangle Park (RTP) near Durham, North Carolina.

◆ At Nordstrom's, the advancement of women is key. Sixty-three per cent of top executives are women, and women manage 117 of the company's 157 stores.

◆ Wegman's food markets have raised grocery shopping to "theatre", says *Fortune*, with their plethora of departments combining foods, a floral department, an in-store pharmacy, extensive bulk and wholefoods departments and even a choice of ethnic restaurants all under one extensive roof.

◆ W.L. Gore & Associates has a unique culture that rewards those driven by opportunity rather than title or the status that goes with it.

◆ At Deloitte Touche Tohmatsu, women hold twenty-two per cent of top positions compared with six per cent in 1993. Ethnic minority employees account for eight per cent of top positions vs. four per cent in 1998.

◆ Law firm Bingham McCutchen counts ex-governors Steve Merrill of New Hampshire and Pete Wilson of California among its 343 partners, twenty-one per cent of whom are women and eight per cent minorities.

◆ Scottrade and PricewaterhouseCoopers (PWC) have had no lay-offs in their history. Pricewaterhouse's chairman issues periodic updates to employees. In one such update he said, "We have no plans to downsize, right-size or to reduce our staffing levels."

Lay-offs are costly, involving more than severance costs alone, the yardstick for many such lay-off decisions. In fact, it is not possible to account accurately for their true costs. The war for talent is a long-term fact of life. The most desirable future employees are not attracted to companies with a history of lay-offs. Conversely, the leadership cost is high if a talented leader has been sacrificed to a lay-off. Morale suffers irreparably. Survivors of lay-offs experience grief and fear the loss of their own jobs. Customer buying habits are negatively influenced. Rehiring becomes expensive when factoring in the cost of recruitment and retraining. It is axiomatic that lay-offs add no corporate strategic value important to shareholders.

As we've noted, accounting standards are totally inadequate to measure employee goodwill, employee and customer relations, as well as intellectual property and patents. They are also inadequate to measure the real costs of lay-offs. Even though accountants cannot empirically measure all the true costs of lay-offs, they are more costly than anyone realizes, especially over the long term. Biscuitville, like many private companies, is all about the long-term. Together with other companies on *Fortune's* list, it earns kudos for sensitivity to this extremely emotional issue and costly business practice.

Like most of the *Fortune* 100 Best Companies to Work For®, Biscuitville has never had a mass lay-off in its entire forty-three-year history. Only as a last resort does a company consider lay-offs. Typically, a hiring freeze is considered first, followed by wage freezes, then a shortened workweek and, as a last resort, reduced wages across the board. Biscuitville's "people first" is a long-term commitment.

What all of these companies have in common is an emphasis on employee relations and acknowledgement of the bond among employees. It is important to management to understand and respect the fact that a large part of an employee's life is devoted to their work. The paycheck they take home is what gives them shelter, feeds their families, funds the kids' college educations, and pays for leisure time.

Like many on the *Fortune* 100 list, Biscuitville continually solicits employees' ideas throughout the company to improve its products and the delivery of its customer service. Employee concerns are listened to and considered by management both formally and informally (MBWA).

The absolute key to Biscuitville's success is an intangible. No dollar value can be placed on it. As Biscuitville's employee count grows to over a thousand, as it is expected to do in 2010, it will be mentioned in the same breath as the *Fortune* Best Companies, not only because of competitive pay, perquisite packages, and no lay-offs, but also because of attention paid to its employees' psychological needs. Biscuitville's "people first" philosophy sets it apart among its peers.

New research discussed in earlier chapters has shown that the classic theory proposed by Abraham Maslow in his 1943 paper, "A Theory of Human Motivation", placed too much emphasis on people's physiological needs, such as the need to earn wages and to have secure shelter. In fact, a changing workplace has dictated that today – sixty-seven years after Maslow's study – psychological needs are more important.

Maslow's pronounced emphasis on the paycheck has been eroded over the years as business modernizes. Intangible factors like the need for greater self-esteem that comes from having done a good job, the desire to improve one's skills, obtain more professional education, make meaningful contributions at work and in society, and self-actualization both inside and outside the workplace are what make the *Fortune* 100 companies such desirable places to work.

Employee learning is a vital component of an on-going effort to keep employees abreast of developments in Biscuitville's future growth plans. Cross training is encouraged and is important for employee advancement within the company. The idea is to make employees better professionals. Sometimes that means an employee could be hired away by a third party, but that's a risk Biscuitville is willing to take in order to serve the important psychological needs of its valued employees. Employees want to know they make a positive impact on society by what they do, whether the product or service carries their personal stamp, and how it benefits mankind. Causes, not institutions or mighty corporations, motivate employees at every level. Workers simply want to be happy and make others happy by what they contribute, while earning a good wage in the process.

Only by putting into practice the many motivational techniques that Biscuitville and the *Fortune* 100 companies practice daily can a company hope to gain the most important business asset of all: HEE, or the Highly Engaged Employee. The HEE is not recognized by either GAAP (Generally Accepted

Accounting Principles) or by IFRS (International Financial Reporting Standards), the financial reporting system that is quickly becoming the world standard. HEE could become the most important acronym in business.

Is it any small wonder then that so many businesses should be clueless about the long-term importance of the human resource as an asset of a corporation? It is nigh impossible to apply the critical return on investment matrix when neither the numerator nor denominator takes this important asset into account. Nowhere is the crucial element of human capital factored into the financial statement or accounting lexicon.

Biscuitville and the *Fortune* 100 Best Companies to Work For®, on the other hand, demonstrate that the human resource is more valuable than any other asset a corporation has. It is to be valued over the long term, invested in, nurtured, and respected.

Life, after all, is not *measured* by the number of breaths one takes on earth but rather by the moments that take one's breath away, personally and professionally. Little giant Biscuitville and the *Fortune* 100 Best Companies to Work For® give their employees the opportunity to delight in those moments when they come along.

Chapter 13

Avoiding the train wreck

Succession planning ranks as one of the top strategic decisions made by any company. CEO turnover in public companies is an astonishing five years, roughly equivalent to head coaching jobs in the NFL. The author Joseph L. Bower, Donald L. Kirk Professor of Business Administration at Duke University in Durham, North Carolina, and The Baker Foundation Professor at Harvard Business School, concludes that "Corporate succession as it is currently practiced is a disaster."

He then asks, "Why are these train wrecks happening?" Even though the board has absolute responsibility for corporate succession process, he found the style of an incumbent CEO to be the number one problem. CEOs "cow and break a whole generation of their most talented subordinates." Instead of seeing succession planning as an opportunity, some CEOs "find the prospect of succession depressing, signaling failure or organizational death." Still others who do plan for succession do it "in such an imperial, overbearing fashion that the potential crop of leaders withers in the shade." Some incumbent chief executives, he goes on, "also fear being surpassed."

Another problem, notes Bower, is managing purely for high performance and "paying and promoting those who deliver, while firing those who don't. But often these are companies that pride themselves on paying and promoting those who deliver, while firing those who don't ... they turn out to be companies that think developing general managers is a waste of time, human relations an administrative task to be delegated and then ignored, and succession what you worry about the year before the CEO retires." In other words, it is the kind of performance that is not sustainable, due to lack of continuity in leadership at the top.

The average "life" of a CEO chosen from outside a company is three years. Business is becoming increasingly more complex and the need for leadership more critical. Efficiency, innovation, and especially the need to focus on the customer are all necessary for sustained success. With turnover at the top increasing, American companies are, says Professor Bower, "in the throes of a succession crisis."

The Biscuitville way of succession

Biscuitville, however, has avoided this crisis, and the key to its success lies in Bower's clear assertion that "One constant associated with companies that can sustain high performance is that they manage succession well." How have they done this? Bower has the answer: "You begin twenty years earlier and you develop a cadre of outstanding people who can do a really good job. You can't develop great CEOs overnight. It takes a lot of time. Maybe it's not twenty, but it's ten anyway. And you also have to have a company that's making good products."

Burney occupied multiple management positions within the company, among them manager of operations, director of site location, and finally CFO. He would spend time getting to know the company and how it operated. He would get to know its people and he would mingle with its customers. He would learn how to make its product and learn how to make it better, if that was possible. He would get to know the Biscuitville of his father but he would also bring to his tasks his own ideas for the future of the company.

Both father and son thought this type of hands-on, on-the-job, trial-by-fire learning would be the true test of Burney's management capabilities. Both knew full well that, in the wise words of an old adage, "Acorns don't grow well in the shadow of great oaks." So Maurice set Burney on his way to learn the company from the inside out. He scored well in the challenge of picking store locations, which is a particularly cost-prohibitive decision to reverse when a misjudgment is made. There was no guesswork. After much hard work and many trials, Burney won his CEO badge! Maurice Neuborne Jennings, Jr., inherited his father's name by birth; he earned his father's title through hard work and singular management talent. Burney's ability to turn the crank and manage operations is the skill set needed today as much as Maurice's hard-driving entrepreneurial spirit was needed in 1975. He understands Biscuitville's culture, capabilities, technologies, and operations, and is keenly aware of its competitors. He has a deep and abiding respect for the company's greatest resource – its people. He maintains an objective view of its future while revering its past. Along with him, Burney has groomed an entire cadre of regional managers, most of whom have grown up professionally within the company and share the company's values.

CEO succession by public companies is failing on a large scale in America, but not at Biscuitville. Maurice and Burney Jennings broke the process into a series of baby steps. Maurice gave Burney the opportunity to learn the company from the inside out and trusted him to manage operations throughout. Companies in the public domain could profit from Biscuitville's example by sending their CEO candidates to head important business units as part of their succession planning process. An overseas business unit would be easiest to judge since it is less tethered to the head office. It is well documented in the business management literature that CEOs recruited from outside a company are more likely to fail.

How the Jenningses successfully devised a plan to groom succession from within is an invaluable example of good succession planning. Their common sense approach to grooming the next CEO, if adopted by certain public companies, could potentially save those companies millions of dollars and keep the corporate train smoothly chugging down the succession track.

Chapter 14

The tyranny of the short term

Ability to consider business decisions with a view to the long term is the premier reason why private ownership captures the high ground. All public company C-suite executives live and die by quarterly earnings. The mantra is, "What have you done for me lately?" It is the tyranny of the short term; it terrorizes the mind of public company CEOs, especially in the world of earnings guidance.

As we saw in the previous chapter, tenure for public company CEOs in America is around five years. It is not surprising that these CEOs are fixated on the short term. Compared to twenty years ago when CEO's were usually "lifers", today's boards start visualizing CEOs packing their suitcases not long after they've arrived. Nevertheless, firing is still not a spur of the moment reflex. Even the unimaginative can therefore understand why the public company CEO is fixated on the next quarter's results. The long term is beyond his or her potentially very short tenure. The memo embedded with a heavy-duty staple gun in the forehead of the public company CEO says, "Beware of the results of the quarter where guidance was announced."

The most important corporate decisions need to be made in the context of the long term. The weightiest board-level decisions such as strategy, brand-building, acquisitions, corporate values, and human resources play out over a lengthier time horizon. It is fair to say all CEOs try to take the long view into account, but the bell of the upcoming quarter tolls mightily.

Ignoring the long term is the root cause of the 2008 collapse of Wall Street, pure and simple – the great unwinding of twenty-to-one leveraging. On February 24, 2009, President Obama said it best when he lamented that Americans for too long had sacrificed long-term good for short-term gain. The President has frequently been heard to say, "My job is to take the long view." In another speech in February, 2009, he said, "In fact, you can argue a lot of the problems we're in have to do with everybody planning based on one-day market reactions, or three month market reactions, and as a consequence, nobody was taking the long view."

Michael Lewis and David Einhorn, while bemoaning Moody's and Standard & Poor's short-term outlooks, wrote in a January, 2009 *New York Times* article, "If you work for the enforcement division of the SEC [Securities and Exchange Commission], you probably know in the back of your mind, and in the front too, that if you maintain good relations with Wall Street, you might be paid huge sums of money to be employed by it." The bond issuer, after all, pays the bond rating services.

The CEOs of public companies, especially financial institutions, are focused on the short term, as reported in annual 10K and quarterly 10Q filings with the SEC. Corporate executives are compensated in some meaningful way with stock options designed to bet the ranch on the short term: "a big run up in my company's stock price, I win; a big fall off in price, I don't lose anything." The tyranny of the short term, as many much less wealthy investors have so stunningly learned, leaves the shareholders' holding the empty bag.

The value of long-term thinking afforded to private companies like Biscuitville, on the other hand, is easily embraced. The shareholders of Biscuitville are rewarded by management's long view and their efforts to pay lower taxes. The ultimate absurdity is that public company CEOs punish shareholders by paying more state and federal taxes in their efforts to pump up earnings per share (EPS) and dump personal stock options. So Biscuitville, as a private company, and all other little giant private companies, can filter out the short-term noise to the pecuniary benefit of the shareholders.

Another reason private companies like Biscuitville trump the 20,000 publicly owned companies in the United States is the minimum $2 to $3 million cash cost for even the smallest public company to comply with the requirements of the Sarbanes–Oxley Act (SOX). Cash cost includes direct cost traceable through the check register. This cost excludes the management and board involvement in overseeing and complying with onerous SOX requirements and in orchestrating SEC filings.

The advantages of SOX without the cost

Even though private companies are not subject to the rigorous requirements of SOX, Biscuitville, Kohler, and other successful small private companies have voluntarily established boards of directors which have incorporated some best practices in an effort to encourage effective corporate governance. Progressive private companies have voluntarily implemented parts of section 404 of SOX concerning internal auditing. Cherry-picking the best directives in section 404 allows private companies to operate on more current financial numbers, not ancient history. More timely financial data allow companies like Biscuitville better to steer clear of rocky shoals.

Biscuitville has opted for a board of advisors populated by business luminaries who voluntarily use parts of the SOX playbook and eschew SOX-box-checking perfunctory requirements. Biscuitville's advisory board functions identically to a statutory board, including board terms and board fees paid. The Biscuitville board of advisors operates without the weighty legal liability of a statutory board of directors. It is instructive to review how the Biscuitville Advisory Board deals with important subject matter. First, strategy oversight is placed early on the agenda, compared with some public companies that place strategy oversight last, if it is placed on the agenda at all. Placement at the end means that a strategy discussion commences as board members are closing their board books and heading out the door.

Biscuitville expects all advisors to read their board books, including strategy items, in advance of the meeting. It expects all advisors to be knowledgeable about and conversant with the quick-service business and how their company fits into the over $120 billion a year industry. Unlike the corporate mission, which is kin to the one-year budget, strategy is what you want to be when you grow up. Well-conceived strategy can be the largest contribution to shareholder worth.

Management is responsible for the strategic plan. The board of advisors is responsible for major assumptions, process, and implementation. Strategy and process are mentally taxing, but the rewards are great. After all, a pearl is a combination of calcium and protein produced when a foreign material is trapped in the oyster – irritating when being formed but beautiful and often of great price when polished. Strategy is a professional approach, which yields much value to Biscuitville shareholders. Biscuitville has a balance sheet made of some serious steel because they manage risk well.

Preservation of the people-first culture is Biscuitville's North Star. Until now, new store expansion had been limited to sites within a ninety-minute ride of Biscuitville headquarters. All but seven stores are within an hour's drive from headquarters. Future growth has expanded that radius to a two-hour drive, further than before but still within reasonable range to maintain closeness to the mother ship. The current thinking is that all new stores will continue to be company owned. Both franchising and distance have been shown to be detrimental to employee relations. It dilutes the management–crew bond. The company's current strategy of expanding internally without franchising, and keeping all new stores within a one-day drive, recognizes the importance of employees and the integral role they have played in the company's enormous

success. There is ample room for growth in expanding the
distance radii, since all fifty-three stores are currently within
the two-hour distance from headquarters in Greensboro, North
Carolina.

This would preserve the sustainable competitive advantage of
super service with quality offerings achieved through the core
people-first philosophy. A true employee–family atmosphere
and practice can be maintained. Franchising, diverse
geography, and a larger employee base are policy decisions for
the future. But the more the steady six to ten per cent growth
can readily be achieved with the return-in-one-day future
footprint as management continues to strengthen its
employee fidelity.

Even though much has been written and said about
committees to audit public companies' attention to risk, the
results have been unsatisfactory. The deep recession in 2008
exposed the deficiency of the risk assessment process of many
prominent public companies. The bankruptcy of venerable
Lehman Brothers and the lifelines tossed to Wachovia and
Merrill Lynch soon exposed the inadequacies of public
company risk management.

Biscuitville

Where many thought public companies excelled, private companies managed equally well, if not better. Biscuitville's exemplary, case-hardened balance sheet is a take-home study for public companies. The detailed written minutes of the advisory board, which meets in person, shows Biscuitville three times a year that it has in place a process to manage enterprise risks:

◆ Focusing on financial forecasts and early warning indicators;
◆ Assessment of the company's exposure to third parties in financial distress;
◆ Understanding the impact of any fiscal crisis on the company's financials – particularly the balance sheet;
◆ Help in preparing the company for change;
◆ Asking the right questions and challenging management;
◆ Monitoring the tone of leadership and throughout the organization.

In 1993, when Jeff May was first named CFO after being in public accounting for eleven years, he asked CEO Maurice Jennings what he expected him to achieve as Biscuitville's risk management architect. Jennings' answer was simple yet profound: survival for his company, with a unique twist. Maurice, a staunch proponent of personal responsibility, was determined that Biscuitville would pay for its own mistakes. His philosophy was "When we can afford to take the risk, we will save the premium" and self-insure. Otherwise, Biscuitville would secure catastrophic coverage.

Biscuitville's current risk-management policy is exemplary and is centered on Maurice's philosophy. It was developed by Jeff May in conjunction with Maurice and Biscuitville's shareholders, and is reviewed and refined as needed with the ongoing advice of the company's advisory board.

With 941 employees in fifty-three locations, Worker's Compensation was and still is the company's greatest insurance cost. In 2000 Biscuitville became a part of its own insurance company through a group captive. Captive insurance is essentially an "in-house" insurance company with a limited purpose and is not available to the general public. This alternative form of risk management is becoming a more practical and popular means through which companies can protect themselves financially while having more control over how they are insured. Burney concluded after one meeting, "Sign us up."

Jeff May's financial and risk management of the company as CFO has reflected Maurice's vision and philosophy, and by staying true to his mandate, Biscuitville has survived quite nicely.

Employee-relation advantages over public companies

Radical times require radical actions. Today, all organizations need to rethink their future. This is especially true in corporate personnel. The value of the human resource (HR) asset is traditionally underrated because the concept is soft and difficult to measure in the short term. Even though it is a company's major asset, nowhere does HR appear on the balance sheet. Biscuitville is a textbook case-study of the importance of effective HR.

At Biscuitville, a long view of the HR investment is largely responsible for its success. The company is assured of its sustainable competitive advantage over the long term so long as it continues investing in the people-first philosophy, which in turn dramatically converts into outstanding customer service. Remember, fellow employees are treated with respect, and the Biscuitville twist is that the customer is treated as co-workers treat one another. This investment in people first requires long-term commitment. It also requires cash, not just nifty-sounding words and the occasional ice-cream social. Better that there be no human relations program whatsoever than empty gestures and lip-service given in fits and starts . The reasons for an HR wake-up call during these radical times are three-fold:

1. High touch is much more important in today's high-tech, fast-paced world. The acceleration of change itself has business people on edge.
2. HR has the highest investment returns. Unfortunately, many business managers, especially public company C-level executives, have acute next-quarter attention-deficit disorder.
3. Because HR investment is long-term, expect modest returns in initial years but great rewards over time.

Biscuitville is the shining HR citadel on the hill built over forty-three years by a hugely successful philosophy of people first.

HR trench warfare

The importance of employee human relations is under-appreciated and the first to be ignored at times of crisis like the 2008 and 2009 financial meltdown. One only needs to reference the company's historical record of success to see the dividends of management's serious long-term commitment to the Biscuitville family. Biscuitville's outstanding customer service begins with the Golden Rule: treat fellow employees, regardless of chain-of-command or rank, with respect. Extraordinary service, when done as Biscuitville does it, is the only sustainable competitive advantage any company possesses anywhere, anytime, during any business cycle.

Biotechnology and microelectronic companies have an absolutely false belief that they will achieve this competitive Holy Grail. But limited patent life and new technologies leap-frogging even the newest innovations means that their advantage is not and never will be sustainable. Buyers will follow new technologies every time: witness the iPod and iPhone. But in service industries, outstanding service is everything, and Biscuitville is the grand master.

The Biscuitville "Way" will help all companies move to a higher level. Because it requires a long-term commitment, public companies will frequently find it too challenging to adopt Biscuitville's ingrained habits. The siren song of quarterly and yearly earnings guidance is too compelling. But if corporations were ever to take an injection of common sense, here is what would make up a dose of the "Way":

◆ Open communication at all levels of the company. It has been said, "Less is more." Not so when it comes to keeping communication channels open.

◆ Employees who fully understand and subscribe to the company's mission and goals.

◆ Management who listen intently to their employees.

◆ Emphasis on psychological needs of employees (self-esteem, learning, and job fulfillment) rather than just pay and benefits; Maslow was wrong. His 1954 hierarchy of human needs is no longer applicable to modern industrial nations. Survival is a given. Physiological needs of pay and security are all but assumed. Psychological needs are what motivate employees in today's workplace. Biscuitville knows this instinctively and has invested time and money in self-fulfillment, career advancement, and learning, and caring for fellow employees and those in the community in recognition of these altruistic human needs.

◆ Understanding that employees take deep pride in doing their jobs well and feeling they are helping mankind in the process; employees understand the ways in which their products and services benefit others.

◆ Live-the-sermon ethics. The only way to live the ethical business life is to have ethics modeled by management, just the way our parents modeled ethics for us. We know the Sarbanes–Oxley approach of written ethics statements by public companies is a complete failure. What works are leaders like Maurice and Burney Jennings, John Huffman, Jeff May, Darin Bailiff, Kelli Hicks, Connie Bennett, and Leon Simmons walking the ethical life. Within public companies it takes just one cynical manager to render written ethics policies totally ineffective. It is better never to have put written policies in place, because they merely serve to raise the legal bar when employees do not adhere to them.

◆ Employee conduct has brand impact. Employee behavior is integral to the corporate brand and its perception. The golden retriever attitude at Biscuitville is critical to both superior service and positive brand perception.

◆ MBWA. When Burney visits all fifty-three stores at least twice a year and practices "Management by Walking Around", his presence is more meaningful to the employees than impersonal corporate pronouncements. When management takes in important information unvarnished and at first hand, employees know that managers care and are putting a face to decisions. Managers who really know their employees will consider every alternative before laying them off. The same goes for all decisions affecting employees.

◆ If more public companies would place MBWA emphasis on the human factor, General Motors might never have laid off thousands at the same board meeting as management bonuses were awarded, or Radio Shack may have reconsidered before deciding to furlough employees by email, a new standard for corporate cowardice. Talk about destroying corporate goodwill!

◆ Biscuitville is seventy-six per cent female and fifty-six per cent minority. The implementation of diversity is infinitely more meaningful than any equal opportunity policy statement.

◆ Symbolism. Biscuitville's management has no overt perquisites: no private parking spaces, no opulent offices, unlike John Thain, former head of Merrill Lynch, who spent $1.22 million to remodel his digs, including a fancy commode on legs. The vast majority of public companies have the external trappings of office. Consider, for example, that each of the big three automakers flew in their separate private jets to the US Senate to petition for taxpayer investments. They need a new "CCSO" position (Chief Common Sense Officer) to prevent the top brass from eroding brand and employee goodwill.

◆ Hypocrisy of job evaluations. It is common knowledge that job evaluations are typically bogus because it takes guts and professionalism to both give and take performance assessment. Biscuitville treats this with attention, respect, and reverence, knowing how candid, thoughtful reviews will enhance employee relations. Every employment lawyer can state chapter and verse from clients who gave high marks to an employee they evaluated and then fired shortly thereafter. This is especially true of public companies that focus on quarterly and annual earnings per share (EPS) goals.

◆ One Company, One Team. Second only to disrespect of fellow employees is the tendency of larger companies to divide into cliques, departments, and divisions. Like disregard of the

Biscuitville

Golden Rule, turf wars in larger companies are morale- and money-destroyers. CFO Jeff May and COO John Huffman have welded Biscuitville's separate corporate and operating divisions into one company, and one team, "starting at the top." They have a "unified focus on customer service", which includes an absolute obligation to create an atmosphere that inspires employees to elevate customer service to the next level without compromising employee goodwill.

The Biscuitville "Way" has two common elements: First, a focus on employee human relations requires a long view but yields meaningful returns, and, second, by casting its eyes on the long-term horizon, Biscuitville avoids the *tyranny of the short-term* so common to public companies.

If other companies aspire to achieve Biscuitville's return and profitability and achieve a sustainable competitive advantage through employee-first outstanding service, while maintaining the goodwill of their employees, they are welcome to hook their wagon to Biscuitville's star.

Chapter 15

Illuminating private ownership

In the opening chapters, we reflected on the importance of styles of management and how those differing styles are suited to each stage of corporate growth. It was no less than fortuitous that the serial entrepreneurial skills of the visionary founder, Maurice Jennings, were tailor-made to the start-up and emerging Biscuitville in its early days. Later, it was with great admiration and more serendipity that we noted CEO Burney Jennings' elevation to CCT (Chief Crank- Turner) on the merits of his soft leadership style and his attention to execution, just what Biscuitville needed when Burney took the helm and what it still needs at its present stage of development.

Maurice and Burney's leadership skills are dichotomous to the extreme. Maurice was always eager to ready, fire, then aim; a true action figure; Beowulf, ready to slay Grendel, the dragon.

Biscuitville

Burney, to the contrary, is the embodiment of soft power; concerned about actual versus budget, the ultimate team player. Both, however, were like-minded in one very crucial way: they grasped the value of the Biscuitville employee family as a major corporate asset.

Both were and are highly effective - Maurice now as Chairman of the Board, and Burney now as CEO; both their skill sets coincided with the precise stage of development of Biscuitville as an emerging company when the scepter of power as CEO was passed from father to son. The achievement of significant developmental milestones by the founder and Biscuitville's impressive growth, achieved under Burney's leadership, is a testament to chronic over-achievement by both.

If these two remarkable men were given scorecards, their high marks would surely provide a recipe for other would-be entrepreneurs as well as corporate executives of both public and private companies. One need only refer to current events of the last five years and the multiple corporate failures that gave us the Sarbanes–Oxley Act of 2004 (SOX) and the 2008 Troubled Assets Relief Program (TARP) and compare those failed companies to Biscuitville to conclude that private ownership trumps public stock ownership, and ethical leadership is essential to corporate success. Biscuitville's standards of leadership are, without a doubt, a major contributor to its success and profitability.

The greatest invention of modern times is not the microprocessor or the global positioning system (GPS); the greatest discovery is not deoxyribonucleic acid (DNA). It is the corporate entity, uniquely crafted and adaptable for its utility and flexibility as a tool of business. Consider that the corporation allows a business to grow rapidly, to represent both products and services, to change management, to acquire new technologies, to acquire other companies, to sell off divisions or subsidiaries, and to exist in perpetuity. These radical business dynamics can be achieved with different forms of the entity, such as a limited liability company, American C or S corporation, or various forms of partnership.

It has become conventional business wisdom that wealth transfer to the next generation is a primary advantage of public versus private ownership. However, Biscuitville's approach allows wealth to be transferred without jeopardy of having to sell the private company to pay estate taxes. How did Biscuitville, as a private company, seize the advantage?

Limited liability companies (LLCs) provide tax advantages to transfer wealth from generation to generation while at the same time allowing the donor of that wealth to maintain control over the assets until death. The many LLCs owning assets consist of members and managers. Each can be structured like a limited partnership, with members being passive investors and managers actively managing the companies. The concepts of wealth transfer are the same for LLCs and limited partnerships: the generation transferring the wealth form LLCs, making themselves both members and managers.

The generation receiving the wealth (family members, children, and grandchildren) is made a member of the company. Initially, the generation transferring the wealth holds all of the membership interest in the company along with the assets they represent. Over time, however, the membership interests are gifted to the generation receiving the wealth, within allowable gift tax amounts, and the gifting generation retains control of the company and its assets as managers. In this way, wealth is transferred from one generation to the next free of major negative tax consequences.

Corporations can only succeed if used in the manner for which they were intended and not for the private gain of those few individuals who manage them. The corporation is a tool for the distribution of wealth when individuals invest in business, thereby helping economies grow and prosper. Ethical leadership is essential to corporate success. Otherwise, individual investment is always at risk.

After the economic trauma of the past five years, it will be interesting to observe the pendulum swinging towards private ownership. The private entity is, in most cases, superior to the publicly-owned company. The tyranny of quarterly earnings guidance is not in the shareholders' long-term interests. Small- and medium-sized companies are generally better suited to private ownership. This has been, and continues to be, true of Biscuitville.

For Maurice and Burney and the Biscuitville family, success is spelled H-A-R-D W-O-R-K, hours and hours and hours of it, over years and decades. But the rewards have been worth the cumulative investment of every minute. Biscuitville's profit matrices have far outpaced its publicly traded counterparts. Biscuitville's corporate structure allows for more nimble decision-making. Management and the Board of Advisors are free to adapt to a dynamic marketplace and make strategic changes in direction based on fluid economic conditions. Over time, the ability to act quickly has allowed Biscuitville to grow from its beginnings as a small, family-operated business to the dynamic, privately-held company it is today.

Other clear benefits of private ownership concern regulation. Because it is a private company, Biscuitville is not subject to the burdensome reporting requirements of firms traded on a national stock exchange. First, it is not subject to the tyranny of short-term results. It is not required to report its financial results to the public on a quarterly basis, so it doesn't have the pressure of securing better performance from one quarter to the next. Consequently, the company has the ability to focus on a more flexible, longer time horizon, not 10-Q quarterly SEC reports. Biscuitville and all private companies have the breathing space to make sound long-term decisions.

Second, Biscuitville does not have to comply with the extra reporting requirements and rules that public companies must follow subsequent to SOX, which came about following the scandals involving Enron, WorldCom and others. SOX requirements are burdensome and expensive, costing at least $2 million for compliance by even the smallest stock-exchange-quoted company.

The intent of SOX was to keep businesses ethical and honest. Some, however, feel SOX engages in overkill; most know that ethics cannot be legislated, and many more are coming to understand that the high cost of compliance is better spent on more needful corporate purposes. Biscuitville is voluntarily moving toward transparency in its operations even though, as a private company, it is not required to do so.

Some private companies who have dipped into the public trough for debt financing consequently have to meet certain Sarbanes–Oxley reporting requirements and regulations. Historically, a potential drawback of private ownership has been access to capital. Without publicly traded stock, it is difficult for a private company to obtain financing for corporate purposes such as expansion, acquisition, or other major projects.

Private companies in need of immediate liquidity do not have a means of selling shares to the public. Private capital is an option. However, given the economic meltdown of the investment banks in 2008, that source of funds is by no means as assured as it once was. Nevertheless, availability of capital is no longer an advantage just to public companies. Biscuitville has established a bank line for contingencies even though it has never been activated. The company has always been entirely self-financed, the best of all possible worlds, and is insulated from costly outside regulation. How Biscuitville, without any investors and without use of bank debt, bootstrapped its start-up and growth out of cash flow, while seeing an image of a river of gold in its future, is a powerful example for any start-up, especially now that the former whitewater rush of venture capital is nothing more than a parched riverbed and is likely to remain so for several years to come.

Third, a critical element in assuring the future success of a private company is selecting the right successor. Maurice knew one day he would have to let go of the reins. Yet his heart was in preserving the company he had built, and in grooming a successor who would enhance the value he had created over his years as founder of Biscuitville. His approach to succession was pragmatic. He trained his son, Burney, at all levels of the company – personal, organizational, and financial – knowing Burney would be the future CEO of a more mature Biscuitville. Yet Burney was not Maurice's clone, nor was he encouraged to be. The right successor should not be a clone. Maurice was wise enough to discern that his strengths and competencies were different from those of his son. He allowed Burney to build upon his very different strengths and respected him enough to allow him to create his own new identity as Biscuitville's future CEO.

Fourth, and perhaps most importantly, private firms have the privilege and the opportunity to have a more personal connection with their company and their employees.

Biscuitville is entirely people-oriented. People are people, not numbers. Biscuitville's "people first" philosophy is the key to its success. MBWA (Management by Walking Around) takes the company's pulse and listens to its heart.

The latter, then, begs the $64,000 question: Does Biscuitville have a soul? A trip back in time to the late 1800s may give us the start of an answer, when Judge Roy Bean said, "A corporation is just like a natural person, except it has no pants to kick or soul to damn, and, by God, it ought to have both!" Judge Bean was right that a corporation is like a natural person. Had someone kicked Fannie Mae's or Freddie Mac's pants, or had Lehman Brothers had a soul to appeal to, America's taxpayers might be the better for it.

But subsequent court decisions and legislatures have, as they are wont, carved out the letter while killing the spirit of the law. They have attempted to establish pseudo-corporate souls by defining ethics as a dry-as-bones set of corporate "values" in the name of "ethical behavior", and expecting that those values and behaviors would be exercised in the marketplace. All the while, regulators snoozed, asleep at the wheel. Surely, this was not what Judge Bean had in mind.

Biscuitville

To be soulish is to have the capacity for feeling and compassion, to be, on some level, human. As B. Kenneth West, Chairman of the National Association of Corporate Directors, said,

> *The soul of a corporation, like the soul of an individual, is defined by its values .... If a company is run with integrity, the corporation and its leaders are subservient to and responsive to the needs of one another and of others. Management must articulate those values to its employees, customers, and other constituents – and then live by them.*

Biscuitville has a soul, without question. Its abiding belief in an employee family is deep-seated. Public companies typically give lip service to caring about employees, but have difficulty with its practice. The cavalier manner in which employees are laid off and fired provides a graphic example. The depersonalization of highly charged and emotional decisions, such as firing by email and boards making decisions to lay off hourly workers before holidays, while giving out management stock options and bonuses in the same board meeting, is disgraceful, and anathema to human resources policies which extol appreciation for employees. It is a national disgrace and speaks ill of the United States as a civilized society.

Yes, business is, indeed, business, but if painful personnel changes must be made, managers can strive to do so with kindness and respect and only after every alternative way of containing costs has been considered. Considering the human cost is the Biscuitville way. It is how Biscuitville has indirectly strengthened its steel-plated balance sheet over the long term. A cold disregard for the human cost of corporate decision-making is driven by the short-term earnings focus of publicly-owned companies. In contrast, the real story at Biscuitville and many other private companies is a kinder, gentler employee–management relationship. That relationship is what, when all is said and done, gives Biscuitville its soul. And, ultimately, the reward is profits.

If you asked Burney Jennings, he would tell you that of all the benefits of being a private company, having a soul is the most important and the most satisfying.

Chapter 16

A"maze"ing interstates

The Piedmont Triad is one of the forty largest US metropolitan regions, with a population exceeding 1.6 million and a workforce of over 800,000. The Piedmont Triad region represents twelve counties surrounding and including the cities of Greensboro, High Point, and Winston-Salem, North Carolina Biscuitville has its headquarters in this market, and the majority of its fifty-three stores are located here. The growth of the Piedmont Triad has benefited Biscuitville's rapid growth for a third of a century.

Because of its mid-Atlantic location and the confluence of nine major Interstate highways (I–40, I–73, I–74, I–77, I–85, I–274, I–285, I–785, and I–840), the Piedmont Triad was ranked as a five-star logistical location by *Expansion Management* magazine in 2007. The Greensboro-High Point marketing area was also ranked No. 1 in the United States by *Site Selection* magazine in 2006 and 2007 for attracting new industry in regions having a population of 200,000 to 1,000,000 people. The growth of this region is expected to accelerate in the future as it continues to emerge as a major East Coast transportation, distribution, and logistics hub. As speed, agility, and flexibility have become synonymous with profitability in many sectors, a number of global companies have chosen to locate facilities in the Piedmont Triad to take advantage of the area's excellent location and infrastructure advantages, business climate, and quality of life. For example, the new FedEx Express Mid-Atlantic Hub at Piedmont Triad International Airport has already become a catalyst for economic development and a magnet for new business expansion. Honda Aircraft has also established its global headquarters, research and development center, airframe production facility, and Honda Aero joint engine venture with GE in the Piedmont Triad within the last two years, in part because of the FedEx hub. The new Piedmont Triad Partnership aerotropolis initiative will create a sustainable long-term platform to support the region's growing strengths in transportation, distribution and logistics.

Equally as attractive as its logistics, the Piedmont Triad has a large advanced manufacturing industry cluster. This sector will continue to do well into the future. In addition to FedEx and Honda Aircraft, Dell and Lenovo (a computer company) have recently located large manufacturing facilities in the region to access the young, well-educated labor force. Lastly, the high cost of fuel is making all domestic manufacturing more attractive.

The Piedmont Triad's eleven four-year colleges and universities, combined with nine community colleges, provide a strong foundation for research and development, as well as applied learning and workforce training. Two research parks – the Piedmont Triad Research Park in Winston-Salem anchored by Wake Forest University, and the Gateway University Research Park joint campus of North Carolina A&T State University and UNC Greensboro – provide opportunities for technology companies to locate close to university researchers and laboratories where new products can be developed and tested. When Biscuitville saturates the ninety-minute driving zone around headquarters in Greensboro, "We will go two hours," according to Burney Jennings, Biscuitville's CEO. The controlled growth and the close proximity of new, company-owned stores ensure that the "employee-first" Biscuitville family philosophy can and will be preserved.

Chapter 17

Tomorrow and tomorrow

Clairvoyance is chancy, especially when dealing with the future of a particular company like Biscuitville. Even Nostradamus, though he hit, also frequently missed. But deep knowledge of history, facts, and people gives boldness to predictions.

Benjamin Graham, co-author with David Dodd of *Security Analysis*, is considered the first proponent of "value" investing. "Security analysis" is the correct technique for and starting-point in analyzing a current or future corporation. The book proposed a clear definition of investment, distinguished from what Graham considered speculation. He defines the difference between value and speculation thus: "An investment operation is one which, upon analysis, promises safety of principal and a satisfactory return. Operations not meeting these requirements are speculative."

Graham's influence on Warren Buffett as a student was so profound that Buffett later named his son Howard Graham Buffett. Warren Buffett went on to make his fortune by identifying sustainable competitive advantages and analyzing the financial footprint of companies to determine their "intrinsic value", that is, value contained within the corporation itself. It is also frequently called "fundamental value", or that value calculated by summing a company's future stream of earnings.

That said, the first detour sign around Graham's approach to investing says "private company." Using the metaphor of "Mr. Market", Benjamin Graham's primary focus was on the public market, that is, those companies traded on a public stock exchange. His theory was that the stockowner should not be overly concerned with erratic fluctuations in stock prices, "since in the short term, the stock market behaves like a voting machine, but in the long term it acts like a weighing machine." Intrinsic value will, in the long run, be reflected in a stock's price. Perhaps. But will the long run coincide with your retirement date? Insular Biscuitville, on the other hand, is privately owned, has no outside investors, and is not for sale. The second detour sign around "security analysis" says "balance sheet." Security analysis and most business people, especially public boards, put emphasis on the profit and loss statement.

On most board agendas, the balance sheet is an orphan. It is often not included on the financial section of the agenda.

The balance sheet is a revealing financial document, particularly when economic storm clouds loom in the distance. Balance sheets reveal the seaworthiness of the corporate ship to weather the coming storm. The reader can determine if the manufacturing decks have been adequately sanded and if the marketing cannons are in locked position, or whether to prepare for a legal battle over reserve accounts or unused or unsecured lines of credit. Had any but the most esoteric thinkers paid attention to America's balance sheet, with nine trillion dollars in debt and fifty-two trillion in unfunded debt, they may have noticed jet-black financial storm clouds rolling before the 2008 crisis battered the credit markets.

In stark contrast, the management of Biscuitville has always paid homage to the balance sheet. The universal standard is the strength of the balance sheet. Is liquidity sufficient to pay current obligations? Is the company overloaded with debt? The answers to these questions move Biscuitville to the front without the aid of favorable winds or a propelling tide.

As to liquidity, quick ratio refines the traditional current ratio by excluding inventory, the least readily saleable current asset. The quick ratio, sometimes called the acid test ratio, divides current liabilities into cash and equivalents plus accounts receivable. Most companies strain to attain the ideal ratio of 1. Biscuitville exceeds 1 by a safe margin.

Biscuitville, as one might guess, has what can only be called a cash-flow printing press. Even though the company has unrivaled purchasing power, they treat vendors like partners. After all, management knows you cannot save your way to prosperity.

The company has never suffered from debt overload. To use a basketball metaphor, Biscuitville seems to fill its coffers with cash like an NBA player shoots three-pointers followed by foul shots. It has no debt now nor has it ever had any. Maurice Jennings, it will be recalled, started Biscuitville without debt or investors, the dream of all entrepreneurs. Thus its balance sheet is made of lean muscle with no excess body fat whatsoever. Biscuitville's "Selected Financial Ratios" from its annual September 31, 2008 audit reads like a corporate body mass index taken after an extreme financial fitness boot camp: debt levels – 0.0 times net worth.

"Security Analysis", to its credit, does stress a deep dive into inventories on the balance sheet. CFO Jeff May notes, "Biscuitville runs its own distribution facility so our numbers are commingled between distribution and the restaurants themselves. When inventory turns are isolated at the restaurant level, Biscuitville turns inventory 35.65 times, a rate 39% better than the industry." This means Biscuitville turns its inventory once every ten days.

Inventory management is a treasure trove too frequently unopened. Managing inventory reduces the enterprise investment by shrinking the corporate footing, the denominator for the return of investment (ROI) calculation. If the hackneyed idea, "profit is the bottom line", is true, then ROI is the bottom line. Cost/benefit is really what is important. Before considering the final detour sign around "Security Analysis", boards should consider the questions it asks about the traditional Profit and Loss Statement (P&L) in Hubble telescope detail:

◆ Are sales and revenues increasing and is the company gaining share in a viable market?
◆ Are expenses under control?
◆ Are any capital expenditures being planned?
◆ If so, how are they to be financed?
◆ Are earnings per share (EPS) increasing?

Hopefully, a board can happily answer, "You betcha", as they say in the South. When studying the P&L, the most important thing is sales growth. A company cannot, in the long run, grow faster than its sales. Biscuitville has enjoyed above-average sales growth for its industry – not too shabby for a quick-service company not currently franchising.

Corporate Accountability International (CAI) an industry watchdog group, has nominated some fast food stalwarts to its infamous "Hall of Shame" for a variety of infractions, proving that merely following proper procedures and adopting written and signed corporate platitudes about ethics cannot avoid this kind of negative endorsement. It is far better for senior managers to provide the example they expect their employees to follow – leaders who live ethically by the Golden Rule. Because of its live-the-sermon ethics, Biscuitville has never encountered political risks, namely those encountered when running foul of strict federal and state health code regulatory requirements. Nor has it ever achieved notoriety in the glaring publicity spotlight of watchdog groups like CAI.

If the foregoing financial guideposts are a symbol of corporate strength and stability, then Biscuitville's balance sheet is the Rock of Gibraltar. The corporate ship has trim sails, polished decks, and a ruddy crew ready for any gale, the captain is well seasoned and his vessel seaworthy and strong. Scanning a horizon full of storm clouds, his competitors' ships took on seawater, floundering, and some of them sinking during the financial hurricane which first began to blow in late 2008. But a rock-solid balance sheet protects the Biscuitville fleet and it will grow stronger as it answers the litany of questions on market share, profit and loss and earnings per share (EPS), and looks for expansion opportunities. Instead of faltering, Biscuitville "is planning seven new locations, with definite plans to build in Wilkesboro, Indian Trail, and Burlington [North Carolina]," said Kellie Hicks, director of brand development and marketing for Biscuitville. "There are also plans for stores in Stoney Creek and Hickory … though those locations are still in the planning stages." Locations in the Kannapolis/Concord and Salisbury areas are also in the works. The plans are part of a three-year, twelve-location expansion plan, including a rebuilt Biscuitville recently opened on South Main Street in High Point, North Carolina. Forty Biscuitvilles have been renovated – at a cost of $10,000 to $14,000 – with new paint and logos and other changes made to update existing locations with the company's newer interior design.

To weather a financial storm, other businesses, at the board and management level, would do well to seize upon Biscuitville's example and analyze the balance sheet, cash flow, and the profit and loss, in that order. Running a tight ship will bring any company back to a safe harbor when the going gets rough.

The last detour sign around "Security Analysis" stresses a much greater emphasis on looking into the inner recesses of management's mind and diving deeper into an analysis of the effectiveness of a company's corporate governance practices to determine how it will fare three, five, and ten years in the future.

"Security Analysis" puts more emphasis on the analysis of management but not enough on what's going on in the minds of managers. Management not only counts, management is the reason for Biscuitville's ascendancy to prominence. Maurice, Burney, and senior management built a model company utilizing the people-first philosophy. Failure to appreciate the human resource as a corporate asset is the reason why so many entities fail to become companies others want to emulate. The preservation of the people-first philosophy is why the outlook for Biscuitville is golden. Waterstone Human Capital's annual survey of November 11, 2008 reported that "82% of executives say culture has a strong or very strong impact on the company's performance." Although not included in this study, Biscuitville's guidance is that eighty-two per cent is low. Baked into Biscuitville's culture over the forty-three years is an ethics credo you learn from parents. Ethics is not something you talk about; ethics is your behavior, how you live. A written ethics statement with unethical actions is much worse that no written statement. Biscuitville management lives the sermon. As a result, the Golden Rule is a creed. For any company anywhere to be successful over the long term, living the sermon must be the centerpiece of the corporate culture. As one looks over the international business horizon, one is reminded that trust is the key. A corporate culture built on mutual trust is essential for any company to be successful over the long run.

In a start-up, the entrepreneur is the company. The entity should be thought of as an appendage of the founding CEO. The Small Business Administration (SBA) has correctly emphasized that the risk of failure for a start-up is considerable: "Approximately 10% of all firms fail each year. Moreover, most of this failure is drawn from new firms." Maurice Jennings defied the grim-reaper statistics by founding a series of companies. He had initiatives that he quickly decided to shut down, but no company failures. Biscuitville is his crowning achievement. Biscuitville has become a model to be emulated by private and public companies, a shining city on a hill, to borrow a favorite phrase of a one-time radio announcer who became an American president. Maurice, Burney, and the senior management team, with the loyal dedication of each employee, made Biscuitville a model to be studied and emulated.

How will Biscuitville fare in the future? What are the attributes other companies need to xerox? As a child goes from infancy to toddler to young child to puberty to young adult to adulthood, every company goes through several growth stages. Maurice

Jennings, as founder, had the high concept, the parental touch to take Biscuitville from pre-natal to rapid growth emerging enterprise. Burney Jennings is the quintessential "git-er-done" leader who is suited to execution. He has never seen a budget that he cannot turn into a reality: budget versus actual; budget versus action.

And let's not forget the delicious golden biscuit, the centerpiece that has brought Biscuitville to the minds of hungry breakfast-seekers all over the South. Every breakfast, every time at Biscuitville is of the highest quality and is a testament to the employees living by the Golden Rule. Quality is consistently high. The most important reason Biscuitville's future is so promising is the people-first philosophy. It's what gives Biscuitville its sustainable competitive advantage and keeps customers coming back year after year.

The culture at Biscuitville is benevolent and laced with pride. "Do unto others" is a living, breathing testament. It is the platform for the superior service given to all of Biscuitville's customers. It's also Biscuitville's promise to those of you who have never had the pleasure of a true down-home treat — a perfect, fluffy, golden, steaming hot Biscuitville biscuit:

Every morning the sun creeps out from behind the night before bringing light to another new day. But light by itself is not near enough to create the beginning of the perfect day. The folks of Biscuitville start mixing, baking and setting up before the break of the sun's first rays. As the sun rises we are getting ready to hand over a smile along with our fresh, **made-from-scratch biscuits ... making each of our guests' day that much better**. *You can always count on* **fresh** *ingredients,* **friendly** *faces and* **fast** *service coming together to create an experience guaranteed to put a smile on your face. That's our promise to you and the purpose behind everything we do!*

Index